All in the Asylum

The Lazy Person's Guide to Self-Preservation

By

June Thiemann

ISBN: 0615630448

ISBN 13: 9780615630441

Edited by John Louis Anderson

Library of Congress Control Number: 2014913445

All in the Asylum, Minneapolis, MN

All in the Asylum is a work of nonfiction, but the names of certain individuals as well as potentially identifying descriptive details concerning them, have been changed.

*Why upon your first voyage as a passenger, did you yourself
feel such a mystical vibration, when first told that you and
your ship were now out of sight of land?*

HERMAN MELVILLE
"LOOMINGS," MOBY DICK

E-619

A COLONIAL MODERN FOR BETTER LIVING

DATA

Living Area, Both Floors — 1,545 sq. ft.

Contrast and pleasing effects are obtained through a combination of wood siding and brick planter box on the exterior of this modern colonial home. Careful planning has included every practical living convenience in this big family plan which includes four bedrooms.

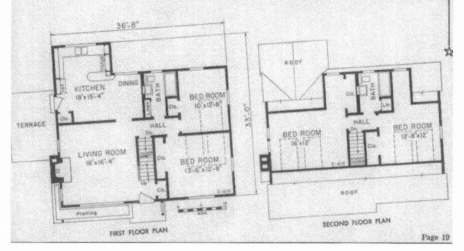

FIRST FLOOR PLAN

SECOND FLOOR PLAN

Foreword

One way of managing not to kill yourself is to spend most of your life in rest homes, retirement cottages, and institutions like my grandmother. Another way is to have a bunch of kids like my mother and pretend to be studying your Bible in bed.

My strategy combined the best of both. I didn't go away and I didn't claim to be saved. I simply persuaded my three, evenly spaced children to watch as much PBS as possible. Then, I slipped away into my study and wrote.

CHAPTER 1

Hold On to Your Heat Register

Early 1960s

We were like other families with something to hide. We kept our curtains open. We took trips to the beach, belonged to a swim club, and had a spot on the kitchen wall where all our heights were recorded.

Our four-bedroom Cape Cod was anchored by sturdy oaks, and we ran free at the end of our cul-de-sac. On school days, we simply dodged a few acorns and did the one-hundred-yard dash across the field to school before the tardy bell rang.

Like other families with a mother in a back bedroom, we wore department store outfits that weren't always clean. We also had difficulty remembering our names and ages. What kept us free of social workers, though, was the fact that our father could cook.

He always called me "the caboose." Whenever he said this, he had a hopeful ring in his voice. I had arrived on the scene in 1962, seventeen years past the launch of our family and just in time for the end, it seemed. By then, Dad was making most of our meals and Mom was making it out to the table on fewer and fewer occasions.

One night, when I was still an infant, the entire crew sat down together and Mom squeezed herself into a spot by the oven. The kitchen was centrally located with three easy exits — one to the "wreck" room, as I called it, another to the adjacent living room, and another to the back hallway and bedrooms. As such, our stainless steel countertops and built-in dishwasher were a mere ten or twelve feet from Mom's bed. But even from my highchair, I could see that this distance was further than it looked.

I often spent my days at my favorite heat register in the kitchen, waiting for Dad and my older siblings to return. Sometimes, I'd leave that warmth and travel to Mom's room to sleep away another few hours. At these times, the hallway could prove a bit daunting. The carpet was deeper and darker and more shadows had crept across my path by the time I mustered the energy to change locations. These shadows threatened to block my passage and leave me stranded in that part of the world where Mom didn't go.

However, I usually managed to muster my resolve and catapult myself from one end of the hallway to the other. This momentum never failed to bring me to the doorway of Mom's room. Unfortunately, there was still a ways to go from here.

Mom was often in bed curled on her side. With her eyes tightly closed and her face pointed away from the light, she seemed to remove herself even further from the world that I was a part of. I hesitated before entering hers. Still, there was something about her crescent shape that beckoned. She was a seashell or a cove.

And it was always warm in Mom's bed. Once I got properly snuggled in beside her (usually against her backside), I'd watch the light move across our secret ocean. On these days, Mom said we were "getting away from it all." But I knew even then that I was the only one who could leave that bed whenever I wanted. I wasn't stuck like Mom.

In fact, I could move very freely in those years. As the youngest, I traversed all the rooms of our house. I didn't limit my horizons. My four older brothers and sister, however, stayed in the main rooms where Mom had once been. They didn't come and go like Dad, who could sail through all of our straits, even the ones in the back hallway.

Shuttling from one end of the house to the other, Dad held everything together. On the night of that family supper, he even had a couple patches of hair left. By then, he'd navigated the tumultuous years after 1955, when Mom had a midlife conversion while watching a Billy Graham crusade in our rec room.

Mom was pregnant with her fifth baby at the time, but she didn't let the fall to her knees slow her down. Shortly after that night, Mom took to proselytizing wherever she went, including downtown. She also told my ninety-year-old great-grandfather he was going to hell, but he didn't go anywhere for at least another ten years.

In response, Dad tolerated Mom spending as much time as she liked at church or in her bedroom. By my arrival, Mom was pretty well fastened to that part of the house and there were no more sudden disappearances at dinner parties and realtor conventions. Whenever Mom appeared in other rooms with a dark brow Dad would invite us out to the field for wiffle ball. At other times, he taught us how to give Mom "a wide berth" and wait until he got home before initiating any significant household activity.

As a result, we were often hungry and stiff by the time Dad walked in the front door. But Dad never disappointed. He bore brown paper bags with enough steaming take-out to resuscitate a room full of famished shrouds. Or, after a little whistle, he'd get right to work cooking up some fresh meat in the kitchen, not even stopping to pour himself a drink.

When Dad was at the stove, it was safe to relocate. If Mom was comfortable and secure, we'd gather around the table. We might even crack a joke or two.

Sometimes, Mom attempted a meatloaf or scrambled eggs. We usually didn't eat whatever she'd slapped together, though. Even when Mom's concoctions turned out to be surprisingly good, they often came with a very long sermon. At those times, we understood very well what Mom meant when she called our kitchen a "trap."

Once upon a time, she'd been a "freethinker" and member of Dad's First Unitarian Church. She'd even taught Sunday school there and made two-layer cakes for my oldest brothers' birthdays. Unfortunately, it was just these sorts of exertions that had seemingly resulted in Mom's conversion to Billy Graham in our addition on that night in 1955. Not surprisingly, Mom quit attending most family and school events at the same time as she began waiting for the Second Coming.

While my older siblings said I was lucky to have a more "relaxed" Mom, I could only remember her laughing on rare occasions. In a twirl-around coat and galoshes, she'd pulled me fast and thrillingly on a sled. On slippery ground, she was more free. Without walls, she could roar with her mouth wide open.

In these moments, I saw her beautiful lips. She was a natural wonder then, an ex-New Yorker at home on the prairie.

Otherwise, Mom was rather hard to place. A first-generation German-American, she had learned the "proper" way to behave at formal family meals and several boarding schools on the East Coast. Somehow, Mom made it through these structured environments. In fact, she overcame her childhood fears, bad moods, menstrual cycles, or "im-ma-tour-i-ty," as she liked to call it, long enough to dance. During wartime, she managed to attract Dad, a philosophical Midwesterner.

From there, Mom plunged into the business of "surrounding herself with children." After a lonely childhood, she claimed she wanted company. But all of that time on her own must not have prepared her for crowds. Often, she ate alone in a dim kitchen after everyone had left.

When Dad coaxed Mom out to the table that night, then, she wouldn't quite *join* us. Instead, she clung to a tiny corner of her chair, with her head bowed in prayer long past any semblance of grace.

As usual, we looked to Dad for a weather report. On this particular night, he didn't make any tell-tale gestures.

4

Unconcerned, he continued eating with good cheer and balance at his end of the table, as if this would hold everything in place.

By the mid-1960's, though, there were several more storm systems headed our way. My three oldest brothers had begun slamming doors, too. They seemed to be imitating the ways Mom often moved about and getting ready to make their own exits from our dead end. In their mid- to late teens, they no longer had time to listen to their former Little League and swimming coach talk of "moderation." Now, when Dad cleared his throat to get our attention, they only argued louder at the far end of the table.

With stiff chests and furrowed brows, they pushed in and out from our Formica table, their white, button-down shirts beating like sails against the wind. Soon, the whole table would begin swaying under the strain. From my highchair at the other end of the table, I knew where all of this movement would end up. Waves were already sloshing up in my stomach and from the grey linoleum below, making it difficult for me to chew.

Like seasoned sailors, my oldest brothers snickered in the face of our wind. By this point, they appeared to relish a good storm. I'd also begun to notice that they didn't look as much like John, Paul, and Ringo as they once had. They were no longer interested in playing "the staring game" with me, either.

That night, their voices grew so loud I couldn't hear Mom's constant sighs on my left or Dad's calming tones on my right. He'd guided big ships through icy waters during WWII but we were going nowhere on that Wednesday night somewhere around 1964. He had asked for "a little civil conversation" at his end of the table, but we wouldn't listen to our fearless captain now. We were intent on drifting.

Even my nearest brother and sister would not lift their heads from their plates that night. Though only in grade school, they had seemingly been through a lot of this weather. Close in age and hair styles, they stuck together across the table from me, providing enough of a windbreak for each other to keep putting away food at a steady rate.

I had no such system yet. I was still in a collapsible high-chair. It had a few safety straps, but these had long since fallen into disrepair. Thus, I felt exposed. At three feet off the ground and six feet from my favorite heat register, I was further than I wanted to be from land.

Oddly enough, though, our house had once successfully held dangerous winds at bay. According to old black and white photos, our family had once featured matching sweaters and monogrammed Christmas stockings. Why couldn't it now hold one last supper?

I saw many sets of dark eyes on that particular evening but none that looked like mine. Accordingly, I surmised that unless I found a way to stop it, our family wind would blow every-thing away, including my own little ship. That's when I made family history.

"Blessed are the peacemakers!" I shouted at the top of my lungs, borrowing a phrase I'd heard from Mom. Within seconds, it had an effect.

We looked up. We opened our mouths. We laughed.

*Opposite page: Robert Edward Thiemann and Wilhelmina Petry Bueckle,
hours after eloping in Ft. Lauderdale, Florida, May 1943.*

I love to sail forbidden seas and land on barbarous coasts.

"Loomings," Moby Dick

From left: Dad, Warren, Walt, Mom, Ed, 1953

CHAPTER 2

Duck, Cover, and See

Late 1960s

Mom always said a breakdown could come from anywhere, but in our house it usually blew in from the west. I learned this one New Year's Day while sitting next to another heat vent in the our rec room.

Even if this was a standard pine-paneled addition at the western end of our house, I never learned that it was meant for recreation until long after I'd moved out. An "afterthought," as my parents called it, it was a room where winds from the adjacent school field would seep in. No matter how many fires or Monopoly games Dad would get going, the space seemed to leak, especially if Mom was out on a twelve-hour walk.

Mom didn't tell us exactly where she went on these walks, and she wasn't very clear about what a breakdown was, either. But I knew that she was forever trying to avoid one thing or another, and this sometimes involved not doing dishes and at other times letting the water run.

From what I could gather, "breakdown" came from outside of the two-story stucco where Mom grew up, too. Sometimes, Mom said, it came from The Great Depression. At others, it came from "seven-course meals." Wherever it began, though, my grandmother's breakdown seemed to rearrange Mom's four-bedroom house in much the same way that Mom's rebirth rearranged ours.

Before 1931, Grandmother Bueckle had occupied the main areas of the house, including the kitchen. In fact, Mom claimed her mother was a "very good cook." Not only that, there were Saturdays at the opera, summers at Mount Tremper, and hired help in Mom's household during the 1920's

Of course, Mom only got in on the tail end of all this good cooking. Born late like me, she arrived in 1924, eleven years after her nearest sibling, George, and twelve years after the oldest, Gertrude. Nevertheless, Mom was just in time to keep her mother company in an emptying house. By then, her much older father had begun to forget which banks he'd put his money in. In this way, he didn't seem to take much notice when the markets collapsed and his wife began weeping in the living room.

In our house, this was the last room where Mom ever spent any time. It was always late in the day by the time she made it here. Then, by the picture window, she'd sit and watch the sun go down. Once Dad was back on deck, though, Mom was often out of her swivel rocker and nowhere to be found.

Grandmother Bueckle, on the other hand, couldn't seem to make it out of her living room once she landed there. It didn't even matter that all was not lost. My grandfather had managed to hang on to his successful spa business as well as the gracious double lot and wrap-around porch he'd provided for his family. Regardless, my grandmother kept weeping. She didn't seem to care who saw her fall apart out there in the main room.

I don't know how she was relocated but, by the fall of 1931, Grandmother Bueckle had gone "away." Pretty soon, other parts of Mom's family were missing, too. In the spring of 1932, Mom's beloved older brother, George, died of scarlet fever during his freshman spring at Rensselaer Polytechnic. The following year, George, Sr., passed away in Kings County Hospital. By then, Mom had been sent away, too. Enrolling Mom in a private boarding school in upstate New York, her older sister, Gertrude, went on to complete her degree at Barnard and take on the family business. In this way, Gertrude preserved what was left of a proud German household that had once featured the likes of Enrico Caruso and William Blakelock.

There were funds, then, to put my mom through prep school, keep my grandmother in residential facilities, rent two apartments on the Upper West Side, and do some shopping runs at Bergdorf Goodman, besides. But when Grandmother Bueckle finally made it out of Islip State Hospital in 1941, there was no one left at her kitchen table. To the contrary, Mom was on a very strict diet that year when she dropped out of college after they wouldn't let her take a senior philosophy course as a freshman. Unfortunately, the one-bedroom apartment that Gertrude found for her two dependents (a few blocks from the one she shared with the older, married doctor who had helped her navigate these responsibilities) began to seem pretty small pretty quickly.

Not surprisingly, Mom didn't spend a lot of time getting to know her mother again. After a short stint in secretarial school in the fall of 1942, Mom put on some sequins one night. The Merchant Marine cadet she served too much punch to identified himself as "T-man like G-man" and had his best friend walk her back through blacked-out streets. The letter Mom sent to "Bob T-man" then sat in the dead letter office of Kings Point for a few weeks. But by Christmas Dad had broken up with his hometown steady. When he got back from a long winter run to Murmansk that May, he went straight to Mom's old apartment. She'd left no forwarding address but Dad found her in Ft. Lauderdale. Thinking ahead, she'd already gotten a weekend pass from the W.A.V.E.S.

By the time Mom made it to our dead end, she'd hung on to much more than her mother had. She'd almost made it past the age when her mother had gone "away on that New Year's Day in 1968." Still, avoiding a breakdown was a full-time job, and Mom was usually "exhausted."

As a kindergartener, I figured it would make more sense if I went out there and *found* breakdown. That way, I'd know all the people, places, and furniture to avoid. I wouldn't have to wait and wonder where collapse would occur.

I wasn't looking for breakdown, though, on that New Year's Day. I was staying warm and cozy in my usual spot. This was a heat register on a load-bearing wall with a brick fireplace directly to my left. It was solid. I didn't have to move to have a good view of the whole rec room, too, including the far corner where my oldest brother was sitting.

Warren looked a lot like Dustin Hoffman in those years and seemed just as capable. He'd given speeches at Dad's church, organized civil rights demonstrations at his college, and gotten straight A's in philosophy. He also did a pretty good Donald Duck imitation.

While I'd missed a significant portion of Warren's life, I believed my parents when they told me it was "uneventful." I could see how Warren walked into a room. He knew where he was going.

I attributed this to the fact that, unlike the rest of us, Warren had been born at Kings Point, Long Island, when Dad was still a seaman and Mom was still a "looker." She didn't mind being seen then. She'd freely posed for photographs outside the officer's club with her new little family.

Mom called it "the old world" and wanted nothing to do with it after moving to central Illinois in 1945. Far from her roots, though, she seemed to worry about fitting in. By the early 1950's, she was dyeing all her clothes and bringing Warren to the family doctor over concerns about his size.

Then as now, such concerns were seen as signs of parental inexperience, not opportunities to begin a deeper dialogue. In addition, Mom was wearing outfits from I. Magnin then. In well-schooled and perfectly enunciated utterances, she asked the doctor, "Why isn't my son growing?" She did not say anything to the effect of, "I'm worried I can't raise a healthy child."

It didn't take long, though, for Mom to start avoiding our family doctor. At the same time, she was feverish to have more babies. Accordingly, the new, suburban house that she and Dad had built would no longer hold everyone by 1953.

So, Dad moved in a different direction. In 1954, he found a wooded lot on a dead end that was closer to downtown. Apparently, Mom was excited about going in the opposite direction as all of their friends, too. She even chose all the appliances for her new kitchen. Within a few months, though, she wasn't using it much.

After Mom's conversion, Warren continued to organize anniversary breakfasts for Mom and Dad and play Little League in the field next to our house, where Mom was now going back and forth to the Christian Missionary Alliance Church almost daily. She always went early so she could find her own pew.

Meanwhile, Warren graduated from high school and got voted "most likely to succeed." Mom wasn't there to witness it all. My birth in November of 1962 had given her another excuse for a quick exit from Warren's speeches and award ceremonies.

Because of Dad's reliability, no one asked questions about all of Mom's absences. Neither did they seem bothered by the way our house was becoming increasingly sealed-off. Though Grandmother Thiemann kept dropping off Mom's favorite walnut brownies, Mom wasn't opening the door to anyone but ministers by my early childhood. In fact, she suspected a plot with the brownies. Frequently, Mom shot out the front door whenever Dad's relatives stopped by, yelling about being "driven" to God. Nevertheless, no neighbors made calls.

Warren kept racking up A's in college and after graduation, he was offered a scholarship in philosophy at New York University. But the "old world" didn't seem to agree with Warren any more than it had with Mom. Before the end of his first semester, Warren had dropped out, claiming he was "exhausted." He'd had to make many long-distance calls.

These were what we called "late-night calls." "Late-night calls" were when you called people you didn't normally talk to—Aunt Gertrude in California, Cousin Will in Toledo. After awhile, you'd get a big phone bill and need a new apartment.

As a realtor, Dad understood the importance of location, location, location. He'd grown up in a solid bungalow. His parents weren't big smilers but they didn't slam doors or skip meals.

So, Dad moved Warren back to the Midwest, where he floated around for awhile before becoming a social worker in Chicago and joining the National Guard to avoid the draft. Once, he brought all of us to Jesse Jackson's Breadbasket Church. He was wearing a camel hair coat and a tall, striking woman on his arm then.

But on that New Year's Day of 1968, Warren wasn't as approachable as when he used to drop his college bags as soon as walked in the front door and let me scamper up to his shoulders or "climb the mountain," as we called it. In fact, I kept my distance from him out there in the rec room. I didn't even go near the fireplace, where he'd once taught me how to belt out "A Hard Day's Night." Instead, I stayed near Dad.

At the time, Dad was a unanimously elected county board chair, who had saved the court house plaza from becoming a parking lot, reformed the property tax structure so that it better supported the schools, and brought new and stunning levels of transparency to local government. Earlier that year, a spot in the Illinois state legislature had opened up and Dad was being urged to run for it. This was the same route his friend and look-alike classmate had taken a few years earlier to Washington, D.C. Dad told a local reporter he was going to "think about it and discuss it with his family."

Unfortunately, we would've been more interested in knowing what sort of take-out he was bringing home. A few weeks earlier, when he walked in the front door with a young photographer, we weren't particularly amused, either.

Still, Dad thought we could bunch around our couch. He used the phrase "as long as."

So, we guessed what Dad was up to. Mom had insinuated as much. She made fun of his sense of civic responsibility.

"*Some* people," she'd say, "are willing to risk *anything* for their fellow man."

In response, Dad would cock his head to the side and sing, "*Once in a while, will you try to give one little thought to me?*"

"Not that one again!" Mom fired back, rolling her eyes like Lauren Bacall.

Even if Mom managed to appear in a matching outfit and the rest of us followed suit that night when Dad brought the photographer into our living room, Warren was nowhere to be seen.

He had driven down from Chicago that day in his green, Volkswagen Bug, but now he was stuck in Mom's part of the house. He couldn't make it out of the back hallway. After several hours, Dad barely got him into his old sport coat.

The resulting family portrait was frightening, but Dad didn't throw it away. He later pasted it in a scrapbook next to an article about his decision not to seek higher office. So, on that New Year's Day, Dad wasn't going anywhere. In fact, he'd just sat down in the rec room after putting on one of his traditional meals of baked ham, au gratin potatoes, and steamed asparagus.

It was quiet, then. Everyone had gone back to their various areas of the house, feeling pleasantly full. There was football on television and a roaring fire in the fireplace. For once, no politics were being discussed..

In the lull, Warren leapt out of his chair, yelling "Oraaaagh!," and flew straight toward me after tossing his full tumbler of whiskey to the side and clearing a footstool.

While I'd seen some sudden movement around our house, I'd never witnessed anything like this. I could only guess from the jagged look on Warren's face that he was not proposing a game of indoor football. I wondered, though, if he might not be having a born-again conversion like Mom since this was the same room where she had fallen to her knees.

Clearly, Warren wasn't falling to his knees. In fact, he was coming toward me.

In many of her discussions of breakdown, Mom had often used the phrase, "Watch out!" She never said exactly what to watch out for, but now I had an idea of what she meant. This quick calculation spared me any collateral damage from the new storm system that entered our house on the first day of 1969. By ducking, I managed to avoid collision with not only Warren but also Dad who was also flying past me on his way to keep Warren from blowing too far.

Soon, it was quiet again by my heat register. But I didn't stay in a ball. I picked myself up and followed Warren's trail of ice out to the living room. By that time, Mom was helping Warren onto the couch. I noticed she'd left her swivel chair to do this. I also noticed that Warren was crying.

This was a very different sound than any I'd heard around my dead end. It almost sounded happy, like the laughter around our kitchen table that night. For a moment, I saw a portrait of hope. Mom and Dad were leaning over their firstborn and the rest of us were forming a kind of circle around the couch. Warren was reaching out. Help was on the way.

Now, everything made sense: Warren's earlier difficulty with the sport coat and the dark circles that had been growing under his eyes. I breathed a sigh of relief. All Warren needed was a little help and my plan was to tell him *all about it* when we got back to our old spot by the fireplace. Then, he would roll his eyes, crack his old smile and say, "Wow! Did I really spill my whole drink?"

Unfortunately, help wasn't fast enough. Soon, Mom and Dad were murmuring about "the high life" and Warren was flicking his head again. It didn't take much from there before Warren was talking himself off our couch and back up to Chicago. He managed to circulate there a little longer before crashing. During that first hospitalization, a young psychiatrist diagnosed Warren with "manic depression" and prescribed lithium. Warren responded so well that, after a few weeks, he was discharged and able to fly around once again.

With each arrest, hospitalization, and relocation, Warren got closer and closer to that bed in the corner where my mother and grandmother spent so much of their lives. But I'd seen where Warren ran on that New Year's Day. Now, I knew what our living room could hold.

Opposite page: (top row from left) Walt, Ned, Ed, Warren; (bottom row from left) Dad, Janet, June, Mom on that December night in 1967.

Attempted Rescue Missions and Questionable Placements,

1968-1973

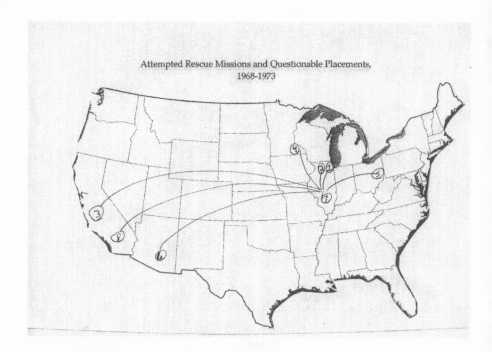

Attempted Rescue Missions and Questionable Placements,
1968-1973

1. Warren returns to Chicago, January 1968.
2. Warren ends up in the emergency room at Rush-Presbyterian Hospital later that year.
3. Warren leaves on a sudden trip to California, leaving green VW bug at O'Hare.
4. Dad drives Warren to Hazelden. Warren quits program suddenly.
5. Warren goes back to New York. Ends up in The Tombs Detention Center for disorderly conduct. Dad bails Warren out after Warren expresses suicidal thoughts. Warren then makes provocative comments to fellow bus passengers. Ends up in Ohio. Ohio relatives call Dad.

Dad gets in the car that night. Drives eight hours to relative's house. Warren refuses to get in the car. Dad allegedly punches Warren. Warren later attacks Dad in the car. State trooper intervenes. Charges are filed, 1970.

6. Warren goes west again.
7. Various treatments and hospitalizations locally and in the Midwest, 1971-72.
8. More visits to the west throughout the 1970s, which last longer but end as all other relocations do.

From left: Warren, Ned (in back), Ed, Mom, Walt, Dad, June (in front). Unseen: Janet (taking photo), 1973.

CHAPTER 3

Touch the Ties

Early 1970s

If the wind that blew through our house that New Year's Day came a little late for Warren, the one that blew in September of 1973 came a little early for Ned. At the time, I didn't see any connection between Warren's wind and Ned's wind. Neither did the psychiatrists. All I knew was that the dark eyes on our dead end were spreading.

But Ned didn't seem to be blowing around in high school. He was wearing ankle weights then. If he wasn't training for cross country, he was usually behind a book or playing chess with his friends. He could smuggle his friends in and out of our rec room without "rocking the boat," as Dad would say.

I took it upon myself to know who was where around our parts. If Warren showed up in the chair he'd once flown out of, I went out to the rec room to check on the conditions. Warren didn't mind my company. He was often staring out the window, anyway. Holding his head in his hand, he'd nod every now and then to, "I'm So Tired."

In these moments, I sometimes felt compelled to remind Warren of Dad's indoor smoking policies. This was when I saw how quick on his feet Warren still was. Faster than I could threaten to "tell," he'd leap out of Dad's old chair again and start chasing me.

I always managed to beat Warren to the back hallway bathroom, though. While Warren could pound pretty hard on that flimsy door, he always gave up as soon as Mom roused herself or Dad walked in the front door. Then, he'd get ordered off our premises, and the whole cycle would repeat itself again.

But Ned was a brother I never needed to run from. I didn't feel the need to spy on him, either. He wasn't sneaking around like Janet and her boyfriends.

In fact, Ned actually seemed to enjoy my company. Whenever "American Pie" came on the radio, he wanted me to call him from *anywhere* in the house.

"Down in the basement?" I asked.

"*Oui*," Ned replied.

"Up in your room?"

"*Tres bien.*"

"Out in the rec room?"

"*Certainement.*"

I could often be found in the early 1970's, then, sitting at my little roll top desk in the bedroom at the rear of our house, hoping to hear the sound of, "*Long, long time ago . . . .*" The moment I did, I'd yell, "Ned!" at the top of my lungs. My vocal cords were pretty good at that age.

Soon enough, Ned would come bounding through the back hallway. Even though he was nearly eight years older and close to six feet, I never flinched to see Ned running toward me. I liked the way he flew into my brightly-colored room. Watching him flop on my hobnail bedspread, I felt a certain satisfaction with all the decorating and decoupaging of Holly Hobby plaques I'd done over the years.

Lying there with his eyes closed and his ankle weights dangling, Ned seemed to absorb every word of Don McLean's song.

Unfortunately, "the music couldn't last." Soon, it was time for Ned to leave.

This was what Warren had done ten years earlier from the same upstairs room. Walt and Ed had left shortly after that for Viet Nam and the Navy, respectively. While I had my doubts about where that upper dormer was sending my brothers, Ned didn't seem worried during the year before he headed off to college. He spent more and more time up there as the year went on.

"Mighty Man!" Dad would call up the stairs in the mornings.

Watching Dad whistle and waltz around in the morning, I wondered why there weren't more of us in the kitchen. I always rushed to my heat register as soon as I heard Dad out there making noise. I never wanted to miss a minute of Dad turning bacon, poaching eggs, getting shaved, dunking French toast, tying his tie, squeezing oranges, and sectioning grapefruits. Like the Illinois River, Dad seemed to flow in any direction on these mornings.

"*I can't give you anything but love, bay-bee!*" he'd sing in his full-chested, off-key baritone.

"No rest for the wicked!" Mom would yell in response.

So, Dad would launch into, "*A little bit independent in her walk . . . A little sophistication in her talk . . .*" Or, if the forecast was better, "*Moonlight becomes you... It goes with your hair . . .You certainly know the right thing to wear . . .*"

"None of that!" Mom usually commanded, sounding more vertical in her bed by then.

Even if conditions around our place didn't permit the making of any noise on some days, Dad would still wave his pretend baton and hum a few notes to indicate a song. This was how he got everything moving on those mornings and made sure I got two (and sometimes three) golden brown pieces of French toast, a poached egg for Janet, bacon for Ned before whisking them off to high school, picking up his mother (his secretary), dropping her at his office, swinging by the Y for morning laps, and still making it to his office by nine.

I never worried about where our family was headed back then. As long as Dad was waltzing through all our dark passageways, light bouncing off his bald head, I saw how everything came together on our dead end. Besides, there were no dark circles on Ned yet and we were getting through a few more meals without Warren, Walt, and Ed at the table.

We even made it through a family vacation that summer before Ned went away. Dad borrowed his uncle's two-door Oldsmobile (claiming it had better air-conditioning) and invited his uncle and mother along for the ride. Reluctantly, Mom climbed into the far corner of the backseat.

By the time she climbed out, she was pretty stiff. She didn't leap up to greet Aunt Gertrude and her husband, Dr. Bill, at their two-bedroom ranch on a golf course outside of Santa Barbara.

Dr. Bill had been the family doctor who Gertrude turned to in 1931 in the midst of her family's collapse. At the time, Gertrude was eighteen and Dr. Bill was in his late thirties. An ex-Mormon with a wife and young daughter, he believed in getting rid of "hang-ups" and soon he and Gertrude were having an affair. Once Mom because a teenager, Dr. Bill began providing "free" counseling to her, too. According to Mom, his main advice was to "steer clear of in-laws and find a climate that agrees with you."

But Mom didn't heed Dr. Bill's counsel. After she met Dad, she headed almost directly into the land of her in-laws and hayfever. Now, she kept a tissue over her face when we arrived at Aunt Gertrude's and Dr. Bill's and didn't take it off until we left for the Carmel cottage of Dr. Gwen, Dr. Bill's younger sister.

Dr. Gwen was an early pioneer in child psychiatry and had become friends with Mom one summer while visiting her older brother in New York. She smiled warmly when she saw Mom step out of the car. For once, Mom didn't cover her face back up.

But soon enough, we had to go and Mom was folding herself into the back corner again. On the last leg of our trip, she really needed a stretch. In fact, it took several hours for Dad to coax Mom down from a hill in the Amana Colonies overlooking U.S.

Interstate 80. Somehow, we managed to make it back to our dead end that night.

While Mom spent the next three weeks in bed, Ned and I played basketball out by the garage. For some reason, he wasn't making as many of his free throws as he once had.

When the time came for Ned to leave for college, Mom was feeling better. So, she got herself back into the same brown pant-suit she'd worn three weeks earlier (which I'd given her) and stayed seaworthy as we dropped Ned off at his ivy-covered campus in Grinnell, Iowa. Smiling and waving goodbye, Ned looked like all the other flannel-shirted, Don McLean-lovers that day.

Since my sister, Janet, didn't come along, I had the whole backseat to myself on the way home. This gave me an idea. I decided to lean up front. Before I knew it, Mom and Dad and I were singing three-part harmonies to "Harvest Moon." Needless to say, we made it home with no stops that night.

As usual, Warren was calling collect again but Mom and Dad didn't splinter.

"He sounds hostile," I'd report from the little phone table in the living room, wondering whether to "accept."

"He's flying high again," Mom would say in her swivel chair.

"He'll be in breakdown soon," Dad would add like it was the name of a town somewhere out west.

Later that September, when the phone rang again, Dad got up to answer it. It was the dinner hour, when calls from prospective homebuyers usually came in.

There was a band of light that stretched into the kitchen from the rec room that evening and Mom had warmed up some leftovers. It was just the three of us again but Dad had to leave this bright pool of light and step into the living room. Once at the phone table, Dad listened longer than normal. Then, with clear understanding, he said, "I see," and called Mom over to the phone.

This meant was still bright in the kitchen, but I was alone.

After listening for a bit, Mom said, "Don't ever say that, Ned! You could never disappoint me," in one clear, adamant stream before dropping the receiver and staggering back to her room.

As usual, Dad jumped in our car again. Ned was now having a breakdown, too. I got ready to go without French toast.

However, Ned's psychiatrist was hopeful and assured my parents that, because Ned was young, he could easily recover from a case of "mild schizophrenia." This psychiatrist had also developed a Youth Leadership Program and it seemed possible that Ned would soon graduate from the hospital and return to college.

Still, whenever we visited, Ned was usually pacing. This wore out Mom's patience, and she quit going to the parent support meetings. Like Warren, Ned paced in loops that grew larger and larger until he effectively took over whatever room he was in. He wouldn't rejoin those of us who were left in the center.

I couldn't see why everything should be sliding toward the margins. Even if this was pretty much what had happened in Mom's family, I didn't see why it should happen in ours. For one thing, we weren't anywhere near "the old world." For another, Ned and Mom were no more alike than Will and Ned, or Mom and her mother, for that matter.

Still, Ned's eyes were sinking deeper into his sockets and his body was assuming a rigidity I'd seen before in those few times I visited Grandmother Bueckle at her last nursing home. Each time Mom and I visited, she'd grab ahold of Mom's arm and not let go.

Like Grandmother Bueckle, Ned's grip on Dad's arm was growing stronger with each visit. By Christmas, his doctors were beginning to sigh. He'd shown little improvement despite a variety of state-of-the-art treatments.

The doctors warned Dad about bringing Ned home for a weekend pass but, when Dad asked how all the pacing was going to help Ned get back to college, they had no answer. So Dad came up with his own treatment plan. He wanted to see if some BLT sandwiches might restore Ned to his old "Mighty Man" self.

While I liked Dad's impulses, I was beginning to worry I'd missed some truths about the conditions that could bring on breakdowns. Ned had taken a National Honor Society and drug-free route through high school. Upon graduation, Ned had even seemed excited to go to college. Nevertheless, upon leaving that upstairs room, Ned fell even faster than Warren.

Then, Ned received care. He even spoke the name of his diagnosis for a while in the safety of the day treatment rooms. This gave me hope.

For it hadn't been all the dark circles or back bedrooms in my house that made me worry. It hadn't even been the winds that blew through when Warren showed up at the front door, or when Mom stood on a hill overlooking an interstate. These were all fearful situations and I understood their gravity. But there was something far worse than door-slamming and dark nights. It wasn't breakdown. It wasn't psychiatric hospitalization. It wasn't even death. It was *forgetting*—forgetting where we had once been.

As long as I could remember that kitchen table where we had once laughed, I had something to hang on to. I knew where I was. I could stand straight under my trees.

But now, Ned was forgetting, too. When Dad brought him home for the weekend, he headed straight to Mom's part of the house.

I'd already moved out of this part of the house and up to Ned's old room by then. So, Ned had no reason to stir after he dropped on top of my old hobnail bedspread. He couldn't even pull himself up for Saturday night steaks.

When Monday morning came, Ned was even more attached to my old mattress. It didn't look like he was going anywhere, especially not back to the hospital.

"Fifteen more minutes," he kept pleading from his corner across from Mom's.

I stayed at my heat register. I didn't want to walk back to my old room and enter that space I'd once shared with Ned. Instead, I yelled, "Ned, you don't want them to have to come and *get* you out of the house, do you?"

31

At that point, Dad made some facial gestures.

"Maybe the less talk the better, Miss J.J.," he whispered from his chair at the little phone table in the living room, where he was beginning to make calls.

I was aghast. If only for a moment, Dad was asking me to forget something, too.

I wouldn't take the hint. Even if I stopped offering Ned advice, I stayed put when Walt and Ed arrived.

Ed was carrying something behind his back when he came in. Sensing this, Ned began to grow anxious at the other end of the house. He was pacing and pleading for "calm." By accident, he took one step too many into the living room. Ed seized the opportunity. With a few easy moves, he'd wrestled Ned down onto the carpeting. Ned hardly made a sound and Ed looked surprised by the ease of the takedown. He smiled sheepishly. He hadn't even lost his glasses in the scuffle. Leaving nothing to chance, though, he quickly tied up Ned's hands with the piece of rope he'd slipped into the house.

Then, Ed pulled Ned up. I hadn't ever seen my brothers horse around, but it almost looked like he was giving Ned a big bear hug. Within moments, Walt had joined the pack and was steering the clump toward the front door. Dad was holding it open like he always did on bright mornings. With sun flooding our interiors, Dad almost tipped his hat to me on the way out.

Just part of the deal," Dad always said in reference to the lengths he frequently had to go to in order to get someone into the hospital. He'd prepared our station wagon in advance, making no special effort to hide this rescue operation (or any other like it) from the neighbors.

Still, this morning was different and Dad gave me a knowing look. After all, I was "the Boss." He knew he'd owe me a lot of French toast later.

But I wasn't so hungry after I watched my brothers get Ned into the car. In all that blinding light, I could see everything — the way our naked branches refused to hide the primitive ways we tried to hang onto each other.

Dad stood waiting with an extra bit of rope to tie around the back doors in case Ned "got any ideas" about escaping en route to the emergency room. Then, he was off, disappearing with his load just before the early birds began walking past our house on their way to school.

I turned then and made a noise I'd never heard myself make before.

Mom was waiting in her bed. She'd had no one to hold her when all of her family structures began collapsing around her but she was now able to pat me lightly on the back.

"I know. I'm praying about it, June," she said, calming my sobs.

As I set out for school that morning, I had no idea who would get pulled out of our living room next. Nevertheless, when I looked back at our trees, I could see that our house was still standing.

*You shuddered as you gazed, and wondered what
monstrous cannibal and savage could ever have
gone a death-harvesting with such a hacking,
horrifying implement.*

"THE SPOUTER INN," MOBY DICK

Dad, 1970s

CHAPTER 4

Find Ballast

Mid-1970s

After a while, Ed didn't need to pull Ned out of the house. Every other semester or so, Ned would voluntarily get up from his bed and go back to college. At these times, it seemed like Ned had "recovered," but I was suspicious. Either way, Ed remained on call to help in any way he could.

Ed had always been a quiet C-student and a natural athlete. He was also what we called "stubborn." As a high schooler, he helped to lead a month-long expedition into the Boundary Waters Canoe Area but refused to wash his p.e. uniform. This resulted in Ed finding himself one credit short of graduation during the spring of his senior year. Instead of going to summer school, Ed decided to sign up for a four-year term in the Navy.

He wanted to get out of our house as quickly as possible, it seemed. The parked destroyer he landed on in the Caribbean wasn't what he had in mind, though. Within two years, Ed was back.

After his general discharge, it wasn't long before Ed became the first in the family to own his own home. This wasn't enough to keep him busy, though. On Saturdays, he'd swing by to install new energy-saving devices around our place, too. "I promise you, this will save you work, Mom," he'd say, sounding like a door-to-door salesman.

Standing on the front steps in a tightly fastened bathrobe, Mom would say, "Whew!" But Ed never let Mom's exhalations put him off. If he couldn't get one of his big boxes from Sears in through the front door, he'd go around back. Watching Ed sheepishly maneuver around our dead end provided great entertainment value on those grey Saturday afternoons. I had my doubts about Ed and his remodeling projects, but at least he was available when I needed help with mine.

We had a couple of painting sessions up in Ned's old room that fall before Ned came home. Ed wanted me to squeeze every last drop of paint out of the roller before going back for more, but he let me cover up those old beige walls with a bright green.

While Ed worked, I informed him of his need for a girlfriend. For once, I saw a grin sneak across his face. It was the same look of surprise as when Dad sent him out for the long bombs during our annual Thanksgiving scrimmages. I now told Ed that if he ever wanted to find someone he'd have to first let himself be seen.

Ed was extremely frugal. To save money, he occasionally washed clothes in his bathtub. Nevertheless, Ed had splurged on a pair of contacts by the next time I saw him. I saw his high cheeks, strong jawline, and soft, brown eyes as if for the first time. Based on this, I assured Ed it would only be a matter of time before he'd have a "lovelife."

Soon, Ed had taken up flying lessons at our local airport. Encouraged by the smile of the receptionist, he signed up for a whole year's worth. When she declined to go out with him, he wouldn't leave his bungalow for anything but work.

Dad would drop off Grandma's cookies, but I tended to stay in the car. I didn't see why Ed needed feeding now, too. He was still getting out of bed.

Slowly, Ed began to formulate a new plan. He was going to become a realtor like Dad. He even bought a plaid sport coat. But after he got his broker's license, he seemed to lose interest. Whenever he stopped by, he'd sigh to enter our living room. Adjusting his jaw like Mom whenever she headed out to the dentist, Ed would then proceed to another project that might lead to more order.

Sometimes, he didn't have to go very far. For example, if Dad hadn't scooped me up from my heat register and spirited me away for dance class at the YWCA, I was pretty limp by the time Ed arrived on those Saturday afternoons. Upon finding me in a heap somewhere, he'd circumnavigate the house and wonder who was at the helm. Mom was always doing wash and folding clothes to the Metropolitan Opera in the basement. She never came up until it was dark outside.

Like Dad, Ed had a swimmer's build. At once commanding and graceful, he was one of the few in the family flexible enough to crawl all the way down to my spot on the floor. Based on this, Ed had occasionally asked Mom if there hadn't been some mix-up at the hospital. She would explain that he was the only baby she was absolutely sure of. Against her doctor's advice and maternity trends at the height of the Cold War, she'd insisted on keeping Ed in the room with her.

Now, Ed kept me company and taught me how to type on one of those Saturdays. He didn't always appear too sanguine about where things were headed on our dead end but after our typing session he told me, like Dad, I could go anywhere.

There is, one knows not what sweet mystery about this sea, whose gently awful stirrings seem to speak of some hidden soul beneath; like those fabled undulations of the Ephesian sod over the buried Evangelist St. John. And meet it is, that over these sea-pastures, wide-rolling watery prairies and Potters' Fields of all four continents, the waves should rise and fall, and ebb and flow unceasingly; for here, millions of mixed shades and shadows, drowned dreams, somnanbulisms, reveries; all that we call lives and souls, lie dreaming, dreaming, still; tossing like slumberers in their beds; the ever-rolling waves but made so by their restlessness.

"THE PACIFIC," MOBY DICK

Ed, leaving for the Navy, 1968

CHAPTER 5

Keep Yet More from Blowing out the Front Door

1978

On Sunday nights after Mom left for church, Dad liked to pour himself a drink. Then, he'd sing, *"Some say the world is made for fun and frolic,"* as he began popping popcorn, slicing apples, warming up his earlier roast, and pulling out a Monopoly board.

In those years, Ed was Dad's right hand man. He could retrieve the VW bug Warren left at O'Hare, pick up Janet from ski resorts that didn't pan out, fix Grandma's sink, and make repairs at Dad's rental properties. Because of Ed, Dad had more time for making my French toast. I ate those golden brown squares as often as possible, particularly on Sunday nights.

Sometimes, Warren had blown in from a jail or a spare couch of a friend who he didn't owe any money to yet. Then, he'd stagger out of the back bedroom to his old spot at the kitchen table. After gobbling up the leftovers Dad put in front of him, his face would brighten and he'd begin discussing his latest plans for law school. Eventually, his gaze would settle on Ed, who was back in his old spot at the table, too.

"What are you staring at?" Warren would demand to know.

"Nothing," Ed would answer, leaning back in his chair.

As tensions rose in our kitchen, Dad would start turning away from the stove, not checking my French toast as often as he should. One night, he said, "Warren's just getting on his feet again," reminding Ed of Warren's latest arrest or emergency room.

Ed was never impressed. "If you're so smart, why don't you have a job?" he wondered.

This led to Warren's lecture about the bourgeoisie. Dad started waving his spatula, trying to redirect the conversation.

"Listen, the best thing you two can do, is to take care of yourselves. Ed, if you think Will is getting special treatment, you can move back in, too. This house is open to anyone who obeys the rules."

"No drugs or swearing," I added from my end of the table.

I always hoped that by locking my feet under the rungs of my chair, everything would stay in place on these Sunday nights. As long as I could eat my French toast, I didn't mind all the wind under our trees. But I needed to take my time. I had a certain system to ensure food intake. If things grew too turbulent or if I was rushed, I couldn't get those tiny squares of egg-moistened bread down.

My technique was to begin at the upper left hand corner and eat my way around the perimeter of both pieces before approaching the inner morsels. These were like the communion wafer at Mom's church. They held a secret inside. Letting them dissolve under my tongue, I felt at peace. In those moments, I was no longer in perpetual and increasingly nervous search of the word I kept looking for to describe conditions at our end of the block. By my early teens, I'd opened every book in our house from *The Wind in the Willows* to *Winds of War* and *Wuthering Heights* in search of this word. Alas, I couldn't seem to find anything even close.

This Sunday night was no different. I sensed a new front entering our kitchen and it was all I could do to hold onto my dinner.

"Bastard!" Warren shouted at Ed from down the table.

"Spoiled little baby!" Ed spat back.

Then, I heard the sound of chair legs scraping the floor. More exits were in order. Someone always had to leave. Dad couldn't tether us in place with his spatula. Warren and Ed stormed out into the field and pushed each other around until one or the other ran off.

Soon, there was no one left at our table but me. By then, Dad had made me enough French toast. I didn't disappear.

From left: June, Ned, Ed, Warren, Walt, and Janet on Grandmother Thiemann's couch, 1975.

CHAPTER 6

Make Room for Arrivals and Departures

Late 1970s-Early 1980s

Of all my older brothers, Walt spent the least amount of time under our trees. These were sprawling structures which forever loomed over our cul-de-sac. We had more trees than anyone outside of the cemetery, it seemed. Some had a sturdy stance but most had a way of leering and jutting at odd angles as if they couldn't escape their own knots.

After high school, Walt went west, east, south, and back west again before settling on a spot midway between our house and Ed's. By then, it was 1979 and I was used to Walt being away. I had never understood why he headed straight for the jungle back in 1969, anyway. But I noticed that Walt looked a little more planted after coming back from Vietnam.

Holding on to his GI Bill, Walt went from one college to another until he had a routine. Once he made the Dean's List at one law school, he'd transfer to another.

Some of these were the same universities Ned had attended, but Walt didn't end up where Ned had. Instead, Walt passed the bar and joined a local firm. Wearing a new suit from Dad's favorite men's shop downtown, he walked into our kitchen one spring night in 1980 and stood behind his old chair.

Mom had been wearing a new outfit that year. She was "moderating," according to Dad. He attributed this to aging, but he'd also revamped our menu. Shifting from red meat to broiled fish seemed to have the desired effect. Now, Mom was *jumping* into Dad's car at the mention of "free" food.

It was just the three of us in a dark, wooden booth on many of those Monday night spaghetti specials at Pizza Works, but Pizza Works was a solid establishment. With wooden beams and hanging plants, it always brought us together on those damp winter evenings in 1979, when Warren was out west somewhere, Ned was trying to make it through another semester at a different college, Janet was still looking for Mr. Right, and Ed was working sixty-hour weeks in a steel mill. In those dimly-lit booths, Mom didn't object if Dad ordered a beer. She was even willing to talk about something other than the Second Coming on occasion.

As part of the post-salvation household, I'd always been free to choose which church I'd go to, and I often chose Mom's. Even if Pastor Bedrock gave the same terrifying sermon every Sunday, I got to sit next to Mom and hear her sing. She had a lustrous, low alto voice.

Dad's church, on the other hand, was full of poetry. No matter how hard I tried to stay awake on those velvet cushions, Ralph Waldo Emerson kept putting me to sleep.

The spin-the-bottle parties of my first few years in high school hadn't been very enlightening, either. By my senior year, I took a different tack and became a born-again cheerleader. This made Mom smile as she soaked my sweaty uniform in the soapy water of her weekly baths.

If Walt had spent more time at home during these years, he might've seen these sides of Mom. Unfortunately, whenever

Walt did come back, he often showed up on a Harley. Then, he wouldn't stay very long because of his allergies to Smokey.

Smokey was the one pet Mom said yes to and she coaxed Mom into our kitchen more often than anyone else. In fact, Mom would get so carried away chopping, shredding, and mincing up little scraps of meat for Smokey that she would start to look a little like Dad out there.

But when Walt breezed into our kitchen that spring night in 1980 and saw Mom smiling, he grew a little reckless. A week earlier, he'd stopped by with his girlfriend, Toni, to announce their engagement. On that night, Mom had smiled and reminisced about her "whirlwind" courtship with Dad. She encouraged Walt and Toni to elope, too.

So, Mom was grinning as if she knew exactly what Walt was about to say as he stood behind his old chair that night. In fact, she was so anticipatory that she began to list all the benefits of a skipping tradition when it came to weddings. Finally, Walt had to clear his throat.

Then, he announced that he and Toni had finally chosen a church. In fact, their relatively large wedding was to be held at a prominent church in only a few weeks. After this piece of news, Mom wasn't smiling anymore. She muttered something about "breakdown: before storming out of the kitchen and back to her bedroom. Meanwhile, Walt pivoted from this end of the house and towards Dad in his old captain's chair at the other.

Like a knowing Walter Cronkite, Dad simply nodded his head and promised Walt that he'd get everyone to the church on time.

Top row from left: Dad, Ned, Ed, Walt, Warren. In front: Janet, Mom, June, Christmas 1979.

CHAPTER 7

Secure Doors

1980

Until Ed appeared in my student union that fall, I never knew our wind could blow eight hours north and through an entirely different set of trees. Ed was taking our wind further than it had ever gone before. By then, he wore an old tan parka and was carrying a heavy sleeping bag. Not surprisingly, neither of these appeared to be getting him anywhere.

We'd danced at Walt and Toni's wedding a few months earlier, but Ed had been going in circles since. With the collapse of the Alaskan pipeline deal soon after, it didn't take long for Ed to be laid off from his job. At that point, he was no longer interested in any form of work.

He'd begun going to a bar called Second Chance and opening his bungalow to anyone in need of a spare bed, including Warren. The two of them would stop by our house that summer and talk about George Eliot, Thomas Hardy, and Karl Marx with Mom. They looked happy and soon Warren had fallen in love again. This time it was a red-haired neighbor of Ed's with two grown sons in need of work. Ed was trying to help them find jobs. In exchange, the red-haired woman made garbanzo bean salads. Ed and Warren couldn't stop raving about them whenever they came over. They were no longer hungry for Dad's cooking, it seemed.

But it didn't take long for Ed to end up in jail. After that, he was in no hurry to be released. When he finally was, he used all of his savings to bail out his jailed friends. Soon enough, he was taping newspaper all over his windows so that these new friends wouldn't find him.

That fall, Ed lost his house in a poker game and Warren found himself homeless again. Before long, he'd landed in a maximum-security prison downstate for a rap sheet of unpaid telephone bills and petty misdemeanors. With Reagan in office, not even Walt could get Warren out.

Mom said our house was getting a "break." In this spirit, my parents proceeded to tighten the criteria for admission. Receiving a room was now dependent on staying functional or agreeing to psychiatric help, both of which Ed flatly refused.

So, Ed found his way to my student union before long. Having learned a few tricks from Dad, I smuggled an extra tray of food out of the cafeteria for him. Ed was vague on his plans, so I found him a spare dorm room. I even invited him to a Kierkegaard seminar.

After a few days, I broached the issue of his plans again. We were sitting in my dorm room.

"How long are you planning to stay, Ed?" I asked.

At that point, it was good that I knew about Dad's other tricks, too. As soon as Ed stormed out, I quickly chainlocked my door. Though Ed called me every name in the book and pounded on the other side for awhile, he disappeared before I could call campus security, as if he knew a few tricks, too.

CHAPTER 8

Stay Somewhere

1984

From time to time, I wanted to spend a semester in my old
bedroom, but Dad made me a deal. If I could make it into his car
by noon, we'd reach Iowa and our favorite German restaurant
by dinner. Then, if we got going early enough the next day,
we'd make it into my college town in time for breakfast at my
favorite café. Meal by meal, then, Dad kept me moving. Pretty
soon, we'd be back on campus and Dad would turn around to
fetch someone else out of our corners.

I wasn't around our dead end, then, on the many nights
when Ed ran up to our front door, shouting that cars full of
young men were out to get him. I wasn't there to see Dad pry
a baseball bat out of Ed's hands one night. I also didn't see the
dead raccoon Ed brought home in his arms another time.

According to Dad, Mom had been very "clever" that time.
She picked up the phone and managed to stall Ed from his plan
to skin and cook up the raccoon in our backyard with calls to
the Health Department.

Mom only shrugged when Dad saluted her. She didn't seem to think Ed was on any highways she hadn't travelled herself.

By my senior year, Ed blew into town again. This time, I made dinner for him. He didn't wait around for me to ask about his itinerary, though. He only stayed long enough to do a dumpster raid and leave the goods on my table.

By then, I'd met a dark-haired urban studies major. Bart had seen me dance. He even liked my cooking. After I told him what was in the casserole I'd made from Ed's rescued ingredients, Bart called it "good."

CHAPTER 9

Become Visible

1985

*While we were out of town Zeller [Mental Health Center]
released Ed to the halfway house on Monroe St. He felt
uncomfortable there and on Saturday walked to the mission
for lunch and then to Grandma's where he met Ned and
Grandma as they were returning from the homestead. Ed felt
anxious and wanted to return to Zeller. He asked the person
on duty at Zeller to let him back in but the psychologist said
that he had been released to the halfway house and that it was
typical to feel uncomfortable and that he should go back there.
Ned then took him back there and left him. I guess about 9
or 10 that evening Ed left and walked around for a long time
and then about 3 a.m. in the morning he walked down on the
interstate near Adams St. entrance and jumped in front of a
car with the intention of taking his life. The young fellow that
hit him was I think 19 and panicked and went on and called
the police about 30 minutes later from home. In the meantime
after about 20 minutes Ed was able to flag down a car and they*

*got the police and got him to the hospital. Walt was called and
went to the hospital with Ned and they operated and set his
legs Sunday morning. He has been in intensive care all week
although I believe he may be moved into a regular room today
or this weekend . . . His spirits are pretty good . . . He told Walt
that the self-destructive thoughts are now out of his mind and
I think this is a hopeful sign . . . He told me that he inquired
of the nurse who was paying for it and she said the state was
so time will tell. He seemed pleased about that so I guess it
is a good sign that he has interest in who is paying. About
the only complaint to me was that the nurse who inserted the
suppositories had long fingernails . . .*

(letter from Dad, August, 1984)

After I heard about Ed's suicide attempt, I sent him a book
called *Happy To Be Here* and tried not to go near any highways.
Fortunately, I didn't have a car.

Mom and Dad had just moved me into an apartment in
Minneapolis that summer after college. In fact, they'd been
coming home from the move when Ed decided to take a walk
on the highway. Even if my parents helped me get situated in
a nice set of rooms on a street called Pleasant Avenue, I found
myself roaming between several restaurant booths everyday.
Eventually, I got a part-time job at a peanut pub.

Meanwhile, Bart encouraged me to see a therapist. This
made me the first in our family to voluntarily seek help. After a
few appointments, I felt so good that I recommended therapy to
Ed during my visit home for the holidays.

He was in a wheelchair at Zeller but he looked bouyant.
Zeller had a smokey, vending-machine lounge, where Ed said
he was thinking about becoming a psychiatrist. I suggested a
few avenues toward a possible career in this field, but Ed just
smiled. He said he wanted "to know all there is to know."

That's all I needed to know that I needed some fresh air *fast*.

At least, I managed to give Ed a hug goodbye. I didn't want
to touch him because I wanted to spare him contact with my
suddenly active armpits.

A few weeks later, Ed's doctors began to talk about discharge. For the last six months, they'd been trying every pharmaceutical concoction they could think of. Stumped, they wrote, "Patient will be ready for discharge after absence of suicidal ideation for seventy-two hours" in Ed's chart.

By mid-March, Ed was being discharged without a solid placement plan. A week later, Dad was pulling Ed out of an upstairs bed again.

On March 20, Ed crawled down to our old spot in the living room and went into a fetal position. He said he wasn't going anywhere, not even to the bathroom.

After several hours, Dad, Janet, and Mom talked Ed off the floor and into the car for a ride down to the new outpatient counselor he'd been assigned. This counselor gave Ed a new prescription and made him promise not to kill himself. Ed was smiling when he left that appointment. He even packed his suitcase the next morning for the trip with Dad he had agreed to. Dad wanted to take Ed to a cutting-edge psychiatric hospital in St. Louis.

But Ed had other plans. During a twenty-minute lapse of supervision on March 21, 1985, Ed slipped out our back door. This time, Ed wasted no time in tying his last knot.

From left: Ned, Mom, Dad, Janet, and Warren outside my apartment, days after Ed's suicide in March, 1985.

CHAPTER 10

Hold On To Your Ties

March 21, 1985

It was my sister who had found Ed. She'd been living at home that year, too. After going in and out of college, Janet decided to return to her old job in the linen department. She'd often been mistaken for Ali MacGraw, but she never liked to call attention to herself. Instead, she took pictures of everyone else and got our birthday cakes ordered.

On the day after Ed hung himself in our garage, Janet stood in our kitchen. Taking up Dad's old spot at the sink, she looked like she had weathered the storm. She just couldn't keep the whiskey out of Warren's reach, though.

So, it was a little drafty in our rec room by the time I arrived from Minneapolis.

I'd spent the evening before at a German restaurant. Fortified with roast pork, spaetzel, and red cabbage, I managed to board a plane the next morning. I felt pretty shakey, though, When I reached Warren and Ned by the fireplace, I still felt like I was blowing around.

No one had made a fire that day. The only person who knew seemed to know how was attending to funeral matters and keeping Mom by his side. So, Warren and Ned and Janet and I had only each other. Walt was with his own little family a few miles away.

The next day, Ned began belting *"Christ the Lord is risen today."* It was after a certain point in the funeral, when Pastor Bedrock had a debate with himself as to where Ed would go in the afterlife. Mom had chosen the hymn and soon we were all singing along.

After the burial, though, we were pretty well scattered. Dad could barely get us back in the car.

"Come on, Mighty Man! Don't keep your chauffeur waiting," Warren yelled to Ned from his old, co-pilot position. But Ned would only pace in larger and larger loops on the front steps. Finally, his circling brought him close enough to the car for Janet to bump him into the backseat with her hips. Meanwhile, Mom jumped in on the other side and quickly pushed down the lock. Then, Dad slipped a little rope around the back doors "just in case."

I was in the front seat beside Warren so Dad only needed to jump in and put the station wagon in reverse. Once more, we were off! But Dad didn't pull out of our cul-de-sac so quickly that I couldn't have another look at our trees. This time, they looked different. In fact, I saw how they might've only been lurching toward each other all those years in some attempt to touch.

Taking to the highway again, Dad's plan was to deliver Warren and me back to our respective addresses without losing track of anyone else. But Ned felt a little confined in our car. Even though we played the radio as loud as he liked and sang every Beatles song we could think of, he called Dad a "Neanderthal," Mom a "zealot," Warren a "professional student," Janet a "husband hunter," and me an "amateur psychologist."

Dad just drove. After about eight hours, we pulled up to a hotel in Minneapolis. The doorman here seemed to know something about our form of travel. He took one look at our car and said there were plenty of rooms available.

Just as Dad had predicted, things began to look up once we had some red meat on our plates. It was an empty dining room and Dad was about to take a sip from his drink. Before he could, Ned shot up out of his chair and yelled, "Get me to the hospital, Dad. Now!"

Dad didn't ask for clarification. He jumped back in his car. Fortunately, I'd lived in this part of the country long enough to point Dad and Ned toward the promised land—a nearby hospital well-known for its psychiatric care.

Indeed, after a week or so at Abbott-Northwestern Hospital, Ned made it back to our dead end without any rope.

CHAPTER 11

Add Weight

Early 1990's

In the years after Ed's death, I walked on sidewalks, taught high school English, married Bart, and got admitted into graduate school. One thing I didn't do was to continue seeing my therapist. When I told her about Ed, she called me "strong." Sadly, this wasn't the word I was looking for.

I thought I'd finally found it when I gave birth to a nine-pound baby boy on November 7, 1991. Holding my sturdy, dark-haired son in my arms, I felt solid. I had ballast. At last, I could go anywhere--all the places Dad's car had once tried to take me.

But I only wanted to go back and when I looked at my brown-eyed boy I thought I knew where. Bart had never met Ed, but he thought he sounded like an interesting person. Still, Bart argued that Ed's name belonged to Ed and our new little son might like to have his own name, too. After awhile, I agreed and we went home from the hospital with "Henry Edward."

All was smooth sailing in our upstairs duplex for the first month or so of our launch. No matter where or when I said, "Henry Edward," in those dark-panelled, high-ceilinged rooms, all the syllables came out right. Before long, though, a few drafts began creeping in. Bart would come home from work and find me in a corner of the couch, with my mouth open and no sound coming out.

Fortunately, Henry was a very alert baby. He had a highly evolved sense of direction. Being with him was almost like being with Dad. On top of this, Bart had done a lot of orienteering in his youth. He knew where to find his true north. On frozen January nights, he simply zipped up Henry in his parka and skated under the stars until he got his bearings.

Soon enough, Bart came up with an idea. I liked the sound of it. It didn't seem in the least bit out-of-the-way or unmentionable. So, I strapped Henry across my chest and headed over to my graduate department at the University of Minnesota. After knocking on many American Studies doors and trying to find the words for the project I was proposing, I began to have some speech difficulties again. Fortunately, I wandered over to the English Department, where I found a professor who didn't need any words. He took one look at me in my sweatpants and said, "Yes!" As it happened, his name was "Ed," too.

Dr. Ed prescribed a cultural angle on my dead end. Soon, I began to see why it had been so difficult for my family to receive help. Just as the psychiatrists had always treated each brother separately, so the sociologists, suicidologists, psychologists, theologians, and philosophers isolated cases and problems. Thus, suicide was different from mental illness and mental illness was broken into a thousand different diagnoses, none of which applied to a whole family. On top of this, nobody seemed to know how to stop the wind from blowing or keep it from starting in the first place, including Henry's pediatricians.

They only saw that Henry looked fine and well-cared for. They nodded their heads when I listed all the (diagnosed) cases of wind in our family. For some reason, they didn't understand my sense of urgency.

But the motherly types heard something in my voice on the days when I needed to head out with Henry to the nearest restaurant booth *fast*.

"You must've loved your brother very much," they'd say as I tried to pronounce Henry's full name.

Upon hearing these sorts of comments, I usually had to leave those restaurant booths *fast*. I couldn't pinpoint the exact word, but something these kind, maternal types had said sent me flying.

Back at our duplex, Bart was taking on quite a few domestic duties. He was not only leading a small non-profit then but also shopping, cooking, cleaning, and perfecting every jiggle known to man to get Henry to take the bottle. Soon, Henry gave in. This meant I was "free." Bart said, "Go." But where I needed to go I couldn't take Henry. So, I found myself flying solo again back to my dead end that summer of 1992.

Even though I'd read a lot of books by then Bart told me I'd never find the word I was looking for in them. He said I needed to do *real* research. Without Henry, though, it didn't take long for me to get lost. I had a thick file of Ed's medical and legal records. Still, I began to sink upon hearing all the old familiar sighs:

> Edward Thiemann is a 33-year-old, white, never married, unemployed male who has an extensive history of psychiatric impairment, but only recently has been hospitalized in a psychiatric setting . . . The patient dropped out of high school in his senior year and then had several short jobs . . . Gradually he had increasing difficulties in supporting himself and became a drifter.
> (from Ed's intake evaluation at Zeller, May 1983)

At the terminal, Mom and Dad were waiting for me. It was the same terminal where Ed had once tried for lift-off. I was "bringing up the rear" in the late, champagne light. For a change, Mom was in a hurry. And Dad had been converted, too. He agreed with Mom that going sockless in his tennis shoes was "cooler." She now wanted to get to the pool before it closed. For some reason, she had lately become fond of daily showers at the swim club she'd boycotted for the last fifty years.

This was the pool where I'd spent all those summer afternoons watching Dad go back and forth. Remembering this, I had to haul out after a few laps. Then, I waited for Dad on the side of the pool again.

"How much swimming did Ed do with you that last year?" I wanted to know as soon as Dad came up for air.

"He bought a year's membership at the Y a week before he died," Dad said, not missing a beat. It was as if he'd been thinking about Ed underwater, too.

This was new information. Even at the end, then, there was more left of Ed than I'd previously thought.

"If only we could've gotten him up for a swim that last day," Mom added.

She was gazing into the sunset, stretching her long Rita Hayworth legs out from one deck chair to another. "Morning is the worst," she added.

I didn't ask her how she knew this. I only told her what the doctors reported after Ed had visits at home.

"Ed improved under your care," I said.

I interviewed several friends and family members that weekend, but I also did some sitting in the garage. I thought I could see a mark on a middle rafter.

Dad had hung some old signs and Beatles posters on the back wall. His headlights would illuminate these as he pulled into the garage each night.

"If you can save one life with your research, it's all worth it," he told me. For his part, he'd made several contributions to a national suicide prevention campaign and funded a discharge pamphlet to be distributed by Zeller.

I didn't agree with Dad's approach and told him I had no such lofty goal. I only wanted to be able to speak Henry's full name before he learned to talk, I explained. Dad looked confused. He reminded me that he and Henry shared the name, "Edward," too. I'd forgotten this.

Mom understood. She nodded her head when I confessed that having Ed's suicide to study was helping me get through motherhood. She insisted I was a much more "matoor" mother than she'd ever been.

By then, she'd told me more about her teen years and how Dr. Bill had taught her what to do if she ever got in a tight spot with a G.I. Later, she learned from watching "Oprah" that she had probably been molested. When I encouraged her to seek help, she just gave her old tomboy shrug.

That grim determination had gotten her pretty far but I couldn't handle it under all those trees one night. I'd been reading about "scales of lethality" and I had to jump up and run downstairs *fast*. The living room was all dark, but I spied a tiny sliver of light seeping out from under the rec room door. It was just enough for me to find my way.

I could just make out a shape in the corner. Mom and Dad were in the same chair, holding onto each other in the dark. They claimed this was their new routine, watching "Charlie Rose" every night. The chair was even more broken now than when Warren flew out of it, but Dad called it "cozy." Mom said with one less arm, there was more room for the two of them.

In that flickering light, I saw what I'd always known. There had never been a shortage of love or high-quality care at our dead end. Ed had been seen. He'd spent as much time receiving care as any of us. In fact, nothing had really disappeared under our trees. We were all still here. In fact, Dad had covered the walls with our faces, smiling and dark-eyed alike.

I climbed back up to my old room. Once upon a time, Ed had helped me paint the walls green. Back then he'd been the one brother who *couldn't* have a breakdown. But I didn't think we had much in common in those years. By the time he made it back to those green walls, so much had already disappeared I couldn't recognize what we once shared.

Now, I saw. Ed had once had a bungalow and a job just as I now had a loving husband and a brown-eyed boy. This was a lot but not enough. Like Ed, I still *could* disappear. I needed someone to keep an eye on me. Suddenly, I knew who.

Me and Henry Edward, 1992

CHAPTER 12

Stay Home

Mid-1990s

After the night when I saw what my dead end had produced besides wind, I returned to my research with renewed hope. At wading pools, playgrounds, and one-year-old birthday parties, I began to say "Ed" and "older brother" in the same breath.

Henry just smiled. Even if he found me in the same place at my computer screen every morning, he'd greet each new day with enthusiasm. In his blue-striped pajamas and lime green cardigan, he always looked very bright. After a daily line-up of "Sesame Street," "Barney," "Shining Time Station," and "Mister Rogers," however, he could grow a little restless.

"Come on, Mom," he'd call from the television room of the duplex. He had a confident singsong like Dad. Indeed, Henry never seemed to doubt my ability to make it down two flights of stairs and out to our sidewalk before Bart got home.

Bart always left a cappuccino on the counter for me. It was waiting for me whenever I showed up. This had the same effect as all of Dad's French toast.

After four years of research, though, I hadn't gotten very far. No matter how I put the pieces together, I couldn't see how Ed's outcome could have been different. Once he received help, he didn't want it. And even if he'd sometimes wanted to never leave Zeller, he also hadn't wanted a lifetime of care. He wasn't even patient enough to wait for a new prescription.

Nevertheless, Dr. Ed said I'd gone far enough. So, I put away my books. I even managed to make some French toast for Henry and attend a few preschool picnics before November 11, 1995. That's when I gave birth to another brown-eyed baby and realized I'd been researching the wrong topic all along.

A wind from my dead end had somehow made it all the way into my hospital room that day. I couldn't see where it had come from. The night before, I hadn't been anywhere near my computer screen. For a change, I'd been in television room of the duplex, watching "Washington Week in Review." This was Dad's favorite show and it took me back to those cozy nights when Dad and I had kept each other company in our rec room.

With the appearance of Gwen Ifill on the screen, I felt warm again. Her smile reminded me of someone and soon a warm wave was gushing through me. Bart and I took to the highway. The radio was playing "Walk of Life" and we were singing at the top of our lungs.

That night, we settled into our birthing suite and waited for something to happen. By the next afternoon, nothing much had changed. In fact, the birthing room was beginning to look a little like my old living room on all those grey Saturdays.

Deciding to take matters into my own hands, I quietly slipped off the birthing bed and shuffled to the adjacent rest room. I knew I needed a change of scenery as well as some relief from a growing pressure in my bladder. Secured as I was with several cords and monitors, I didn't see how I could go "too far."

But I forgot an important detail. Warren had tried to teach me this long ago. He never lost use of his vocal cords.

Fortunately, Bart didn't need words. He'd been keeping his eye on the ball just like Dad always instructed. Unlike the many doctors and professionals who had dealt with my dead end, Bart knew how to find someone when they went missing.

With one glance into the bathroom, Bart saw what was amiss. My mouth was open but there was no sound coming out. All it took was one blast of his deep, bass voice and the nurse-midwives came running. The next thing I knew, Bart was holding me up as I gave birth over the toilet.

Our little girl was another alert and well-oriented baby. Looking into her dark eyes and fine features, I knew where I was again. For a while, I managed to stay there.

CHAPTER 13

Repeat Yourself

1995

I hadn't been able to make a sound to save myself or my daughter in my birthing suite that day. Like others on my dead end, I'd frozen. I couldn't take those tiny steps that had always stood between our back bedrooms and help.

Now, I knew why. I needed that word *fast*.

"Gwen," I kept repeating after giving birth. I said it loud and soft, with an exclamation point and a question, in the middle of the night and first thing the next morning.

It held. I wasn't sure why. I only knew it was the only name Mom's voice had never gone down for. Normally, Mom always dropped a few levels to pronounce other people's names. Of course, this depended on her mood. But, sometimes, she just gave up and used pronouns.

Now, as I thought about the name, "Gwen," I remembered that this was the only person I'd ever heard of who dared to tell Mom she was a good mother. As it happened, Dr. Gwen had also told Mom this in the midst of the 1960s when Warren was flying all over the place and Walt was storming off to VietNam and Ed was following.

"Imagine that?!" Mom always exclaimed when reporting what Dr. Gwen had said.

But Bart only shook his head. Even if he had nothing against this psychiatrist he'd heard about, he made the same argument he'd made when Henry was born. He wanted our little girl to have her own name.

He'd also begun wondering what I wasn't telling him about my trees. Despite all of Dad's grilled meats, take-out orders, and picnics at the pool, Bart only found an empty refrigerator whenever we visited.

This would make Bart restless. He couldn't sit around hour after hour on those summer nights, listening to Mom go back over her childhood. Instead, he'd wander off and count up fireflies with Dad and Henry.

Now, Bart wouldn't let me keep repeating myself. He insisted on adding a few new letters to the mix. When we brought Gwendolyn Rose home from the hospital, then, it seemed entirely possible that something on my dead end might yet bloom.

Me and Gwendolyn Rose, December 1995

CHAPTER 14

Speak With Your Mouth Open:

1996

As long as I could hold onto my newest life preserver and do nothing else, all was smooth sailing on the decks of our upstairs duplex. I'd sleep away the days on the third floor, watching the light move across my bed. I felt like I was getting somewhere with Gwen in my arms.

It wasn't long, though, before Bart had to go back to work and the weather changed. Sitting in my old corner of the couch, I found myself having the same difficulties with speech again. We were also entering the deep freeze of January. Before more of my faculties failed, I decided on a new location, location, location. I got myself, two kids, and two car seats down two flights of stairs for house-hunting in January.

Our station wagon wasn't the most reliable kind but it made it all the way across town one day. The four-bedroom Colonial we bought looked sunny enough. In fact, it was fairly close in style to the gracious stucco my grandfather had built in Jamaica, Queens.

All of this visibility was good. Within the first few months of moving in, I was fearlessly introducing myself to neighbors. I was even attempting meals and gatherings just like my grandmother had. She'd dared to furnish her four-bedroom with colorful china before she went "away."

Soon, I saw how exhausting meals and gatherings could be. My old four o'clock greys began popping up again. I began to grow fearful about opening the front door. If anyone else saw my shadows, I knew I might have to start using curtains.

Whenever these shadows didn't take hold too early in the day, I'd stagger out to the stroller and rush to the nearest park, determined to "catch my breath," as Mom often said. Ordinarily, sitting still and smiling at a distant point on the horizon spared me any conversation or competency exams by other parents. In fact, this technique worked so well that the motherly types often asked if they could push Henry on the swings.

In gratitude, I'd nod my head. I'd made it through graduate school, produced a thesis my advisors found worthy, took regular showers, and could even perform tasks that no one else in my family but Dad would attempt, like flying back to my dead end to talk Ned into admitting himself into the hospital.

Still, I simply couldn't move on many occasions. Gwen didn't mind. She'd grab hold of the loose skin on my neck and hold onto me. In her big, brown eyes and quiet alertness, she seemed intent on keeping me in place.

"Whew!" I said in my kitchen one night as the flooring became uneven. I was beginning to understand what Mom meant about tired and hungry children. According to her, this was another place where "breakdown" might come from.

As if they, too, could feel a little wind sweeping in, Gwen grabbed for my ankles in the middle of the floor while Henry stayed by his heat vent. Neither seemed to understand that I was attempting a very treacherous journey: carrying a boiling pot of noodles over to the sink.

Normally, Henry never made demands but he was going on five and he thought his request to go to a birthday sleepover for his new friend up the street was perfectly reasonable. Over the course of the day, he'd listed many logical reasons for his position. Now, waiting for some heat, he wanted a response.

Unfortunately, he'd chosen a bad time and a bad place to bring up the topic again. He was still very young and didn't have a lot of experience with all the dips and curves a question can take for a mother who's grown up on a dead end. Even if he'd waited all day for me to come out of my study, he didn't realize where I was when I was in my kitchen.

This is why I tried to spend as little time as possible in there. Instead, I'd begun spending more and more time in a small, unpainted room off the dining room. No matter how many words I wrote back there or how many creative writing courses I took at Bart's urging, nothing seemed to get me out of those quarters.

"We'll talk about it later," I warned Henry that night, mimicking my mom's pursed-lip finality.

I saw the effect. Henry's cheeks went flat. His whole face followed.

Still, we all managed to collect around our sticky dinner table that night. For awhile, things looked pretty copacetic. But after a few noodles, Henry put down his fork and stood up from his chair.

"You can say 'no.' You can tell me I can't go to the sleepover," he announced, thumping his hands on the table to make a point. "But I'm going to be like the Green Bay Packers. See, I'm never, ever giving up."

I looked at Bart. He looked at me. What kind of force had we produced?

Collapsing back into his chair, Henry looked exhausted but satisfied. He'd stood up to the wind around our table that night. The desired effect was the same.

We looked at each other. We opened our mouths. We laughed.

CHAPTER 15

Keep Asking

1996

One summer night, Henry swung from a recliner in our family room. He was trying to get a little breeze going since I refused to let my family turn on the air conditioning. I also refused to let them watch anything but PBS.

Bart was at the helm this Saturday night and I had no reason to leave my study. No one was making waves. Still, I stirred myself.

As soon as I reached the1970s addition off the rear of our house, I saw that everyone was where they were supposed to be. Gwen was on the floor. Bart was in a chair. Henry was upside down. I turned around to leave. Before I could slip away again, Henry stopped swinging. He'd heard something from a BBC program on the British monarchy.

"Edward," he said. "Who's Edward again?"

I went mute, thinking of possible answers—the answers I was supposed to have by now. I'd practiced this moment count-less times in the study and while watching Henry sleep. In those moments, I'd secretly told Henry about the uncle he was named after--the uncle who had once liked to fish and take apart cars. Now, all I could think to say was, "Edward was my brother who died."

A few nights later, Henry asked, "How did Edward die?"

"He got very sad and didn't want to live anymore so he just sort of let himself die," I said.

"In the hospital?"

"In and out of the hospital," I explained.

This must not have been enough information for Henry. It didn't take long before he was trying to make sense of my family history again.

"If I got really, really sad, I'd become an astronaut," he said out of the blue one night as we sat together on a wooden bench, waiting for a table at the kids-eat-free Italian restaurant.

Henry had always shown me where I was. Now he took me deeper than any of my research had gone, as if he, too, remembered a kitchen table where everyone had once fit.

"Actually, Ed tried your idea," I said, explaining to Henry how Ed had once gotten his pilot's license and later took Greyhounds and freight trains all over the country.

"Well, if that didn't work, I'd become a chef," Henry announced, thinking of the cheese pizza he would soon be ordering.

"You know, Ed tried that, too," I added, describing Ed's dumpster raids and the letter Janet once wrote. *Ed said he'd give five dollars to the first person who can guess all the ingredients in the cookies he's making. I just tried one--very healthy.*

Now Henry was starting to smile, thinking of all the food this crazy uncle had saved.

"I'll never want to die, anyway," Henry concluded.

"I know. I'm the same," I said, drawing the old lines. I thought I knew which side I was on most of the time, but there were ever more frequent moments when a certain panic would well up. I'd have to count heads again in my own little family.

This feeling of absence in the midst of such a full and perfectly solid life made no sense to me. I was *not* in my mother's bedroom, my grandmother's institution, or my brothers' varied facilities. Thus, I should have been able to put my kids in the car and get a hamburger and ice cream on a Saturday afternoon.

I tried this once on a very cold Saturday. First, I drove across town to a restaurant where it seemed like there might be a booth that could hold Henry, Gwen, me, and the scraps of paper I always toted around with me. I didn't go anywhere without these scraps of paper. I never knew where I might stumble onto *that* word again,

While Henry and Gwen ate, I scribbled. After awhile, they were blowing bits of paper from their straws under the table. At that point, we got the check. Then, we headed to a place that had lots of outdoor activities. I hoped these would exhaust Henry and Gwen so I could work undisturbed in my study that night.

But when we found the playground it was awash with families in matching snowsuits. I couldn't even find a place to pull out my scraps.

So, we took to the highway again. In the backseat of our station wagon, Gwen and Henry wriggled out of their car seats and dove down to the matted carpeting in search of old gummy worms and goldfish. They had strange licking rituals and pop-up voices that ricocheted through the car. I had to keep jerking my head around to tell them to stop. My tone must not have been convincing, though. Even a very stern, "Listen!" didn't do a thing.

Soon, I grew desperate. I was trying to hear "This American Life" on the radio. It was a documentary about a young woman searching for an absent father and I thought I heard something oddly familiar in his velvety, offhand voice.

By the time we pulled into the driveway, I'd had it. I headed straight for my study. I wanted to decode the voice I'd heard on the radio and fit it into my ever-more elaborate reconstruction of the past.

Henry and Gwen didn't understand. They wanted me to come see the pillows and cushions they'd arranged in the family room for an elaborate hopping game. Wherever I went, they kept finding me. Perhaps they had the odd idea that we could all keep each other company on that cold January night, when Bart was in another part of the world for his job.

I told Henry and Gwen to go to bed. They lingered in the kitchen. I yelled at them. They giggled.

Gwen was wearing her favorite green sweatpants and pink turtleneck under a red, wool sweater and purple corduroy jumper. When she fell apart in the middle of the floor, she looked like a beautiful ethnic doll. But I refused to scoop her up.

I shoved the rack of dishes into the dishwasher, instead. That got Henry and Gwen's attention!

They both grew very quiet and Gwen looked up at me with fear. Meanwhile, Henry managed to coax, nudge, and pull his little sister toward the stairs. He wasn't very tall and he was hauling almost half his weight up those stairs. He knew where he was going, though.

I almost walked away from my study that night. I saw what absence had done to me and my household. But I now needed more than Henry and Gwen. They'd filled the space and made me feel alive. Now, I needed to find a place under my old trees where everyone fit, including Henry and Gwen.

Henry and Gwen on the couch in our family room, 1997

But by her still halting course and winding, woeful way,
you plainly saw that this ship that so wept with spray,
still remained without comfort.

"The Pequod Meets The Rachel," Moby Dick

CHAPTER 16

Keep It Fluid

Late 1990s

"We're going to visit your dead brother?" Henry asked during a visit back to my dead end. It was the same tone I used to use on Dad when he'd dare to swing by Ed's bungalow with me in the car. In this case, I'd pulled Henry and Gwen away from their grandpa's wiffle ball game for a "mystery trip."

I even brought sunflower and morning glory seeds. My plan was to turn this visit to Ed's grave into a family activity. But it was very hot and Gwen needed to pee. When I dragged a forked branch over and stuck it in the dirt above Ed's grave, Henry became dubious.

"You want to give your brother antlers?"

"Exactly!" I said, unwilling to let him see how clarifying he'd been.

When we get back to the dead end, Gwen painted a rainbow. With a firm shake of her head and a missing tooth, she said, "S-ick it on the grave."

On this visit, Warren managed to join us. Other attempts over the years had failed. He'd be too busy finishing his dissertation. He'd get to the bus station and find out they wanted cash. This time, I found him at the desk in his old room, separating the good buds out from the bad. It gave me a jolt to see that he began his day as religiously as Mom one floor below.

But Warren didn't mind my interruption. He continued sorting and then cantered to the bathroom in his Fruit-of-the-Looms. He moved freely as if we grew up with nudity around our house.

One day, I asked Warren to watch Gwen while she meandered around the backyard and I ran a quick errand.

"Sure," Warren said, gazing broadly at the day from a firm and fixed position in his lawnchair.

He'd been observing Gwen, calling her a "natural dancer, athlete, singer, you name it." These were all the things he used to call me.

When I returned from my errand, Janet had arrived with her own new baby.

"Was Warren supposed to be watching Gwen?" she asked a little breathlessly. Apparently, she'd had to go all the way *into* the garage to find Gwen.

"She was just here a minute ago," Warren had said when Janet asked.

But I wouldn't apologize or let Janet see my mistake. She'd reminded me of the old rules around our dead end: steer clear and don't make waves, tolerate but don't trust. All those years, I'd saved myself only to offer up my daughter. But I was desperate somehow.

On the last night of the visit, I put on some old family videos. From the back yard, Warren yelled, "Who'd want to watch a bunch of dumb kids before they discovered the wasteland?"

Later, alone in the dark, Warren watched the movies over and over again.

The next day, Warren and I were in need of transportation back to our respective addresses. If Dad didn't put us in his car, there was no telling when he'd be able to get back to his evening swims with Mom.

So, we had eight hours ahead of us and it was already feeling like tight quarters before we pulled out of the driveway. Gwen didn't want to sit in her car seat and Mom kept saying "gitchi-gitchi goo." That only made Gwen complain more loudly. This quickly wore down Mom. She began covering her face with a tissue in the corner of the backseat.

Henry wanted to make sure he got the seat next to Grandpa in the spacious middle of the Oldsmobile. My dad had promised him this. When Warren caught wind of the plan, he was aghast.

"What?" he cried, "Am I going to have to put up with this for the whole car ride?

Dad met his eyes and calmly said, "This is the plan we talked about."

"I don't get it. Parents today are raising a bunch of whiney, self-centered brats!" Warren added with his arms crossed tightly against his chest.

"Not June," Mom observed.

CHAPTER 17

Cross Your Threshold

Spring, 1999

I couldn't feed my kids breakfast *and* walk them to school. All of the pouring of Cheerios and dolloping of vanilla yoghurt wore me out. It also cut into my writing time, particularly the most precious part of it—that brief hour or so when the morning light lay on my desk and I still had a full cappuccino from Bart. In this light, I could remember something warm and bright from long ago. As long as I could get back there everyday, I could wade through any subsequent greys.

Sometimes, Henry needed more than Cheerios, though. On field trip days, he needed me to make him a lunch. There was no way around it. Surely, there would be a snack counter wherever he was going, I'd argue. But Henry was adamant. So, I'd fly around the kitchen in search of clean Ziplock bags.

Henry never flinched. He kept shouldering a backpack nearly half his weight and heading out with a hopeful step. He also kept inviting me to join him.

One spring morning, I said, "Yes." I'd been writing about Ed for nearly a decade by then. I'd lost track of the years but I remembered the day. I could feel March 21, 1985 in my bones.

I apologized to Henry that morning. I told him which day it was and why I'd been short with him over breakfast.

Henry nodded as if he'd known all along.

The garage was always his first stop whenever we visited my dead end. He and Gwen would race back there to see what new bouncey balls and toys Grandpa had bought from his annual trip to F.A.O. Schwartz.

Upon learning how his uncle had died, Henry told me he understood why his grandparents hadn't moved.

"Then, they'd lose even more of Ed," he reasoned.

More of Ed . . . It was as if Henry knew how I'd stood in the dark and looked up at the middle rafter sometimes.

"It's simple, Henry," I added as we got closer to school. "Ed was ill, probably something like what Uncle Ned has . . ."

"Depression?" Henry supplied, helpfully.

"Actually, bipolar disorder," I clarified.

"Bi-po-ler?" Henry repeated, as if he were trying to place this term in the known universe.

"Yeah, it's sort of a mix of depression and too much energy."

"The energy part sounds good," Henry reasoned, trying to find the bright spot.

"Yes, but you know how sometimes Uncle Ned calls us all the time and other times he can't even get out of bed?"

Henry knew all this.

"But depression is sadness, right?" he asked, trying to align his universe again.

"Actually, depression is not about being sad," I explained. "Sadness is not the problem. It's something else. More like a lack of sadness," I said, describing how Ed on the road was still feeling things, struggling to survive. He wasn't as depressed then as he was later, when he made it back to our dead end.

"If your brain is working correctly, you could never imagine wanting to die," I added. "And if your brain starts to seem different, like you don't enjoy cheese pizza the way you do now, you can just go to a doctor."

Henry didn't ask any follow-up questions this time. I'd given him a big piece of information, but he wouldn't step up to the plate. It was clear that he'd been asking about Ed, not himself.

"Well, at least, there's nothing like that on Dad's side of the family," he concluded.

"Actually, Dad's uncle took his life, too," I offered. I didn't want Henry to be under any illusions. He needed to fully know what he was up against with mental illness *now*.

"Oh," Henry paused.

"Suicide just goes with certain kinds of mental illness," I continued, matter-of-factly. I wanted to share my research. With terminal cancer, no one was particularly surprised by the outcome.

"Yeah," Henry said, "but could you talk a little more quietly, Mom? There are people up ahead."

Even though I'd charted a route that bypassed the busy areas where other parents congregated with their kids, I was suddenly more aware of my location, too. As Mom used to say, I'd gone "far enough."

Before I could slip away again, Henry ran back to me.

"Don't worry, Mom. I'm going to be strong like you," he said, crossing the busy street alone.

CHAPTER 18

Remain in Light

1999

By the time I went into labor with my third child, I was better at staying in one place. Upon reaching my birthing bed on that Sunday afternoon in September, 1999, I didn't take a solo trip anywhere. I didn't even drift when *A Long Day's Journey Into Night* came on PBS.

It was a newer version but I'd seen it all before. I knew where that mother was going when she descended her stairs. This time, I didn't go with her. I switched off the TV. That way, when the nurse-midwife said it was time to deliver my baby, I was right where I needed to be.

As if signaling a new weather pattern, this baby came into the world "sunny side up." On top of this, she was fair-haired! I couldn't fathom where she'd come from but I knew where I was again when I held her.

Bart and I threw a popcorn party in our birthing suite that night. All the in-laws who had continued to drop off goodies over the years formed a circle around my bed just before the ten p.m. news. For once, I stayed in the center.

"W . . . i . . . l . . . h . . . e . . . l . . . m . . . i . . . n . . . a," I began stammering the next day. It was my latest attempt to dive back under my trees and pull out the most secret name yet.

Before conditions could deteriorate further, Bart had another idea. He said I couldn't keep taking shortcuts and that I'd already spent a good chunk of my life renaming things so I wouldn't have to look at them too closely.

I nodded my head. I could see where I'd gone again. So, Bart suggested a few less letters this time and we waltzed home from the hospital with Willa Alice in tow. The rest of September was very balmy. Bart and I spent the remainder of his parental leave on the same couch. Coming home from preschool and second grade each day, Gwen and Henry looked surprised to see everyone there. They didn't seem to know how much our cushions could hold. Nevertheless, they didn't waste any time wondering if they could hold more.

But Mom was skittish about my house. If Dad talked her into a brief visit to my part of the world, she insisted on staying elsewhere and "not adding *any* pressure."

In some ways, I was relieved by Mom's inabilities. Just as it had been much easier to tell my school friends and their mothers that Mom was "a reader" so, too, I could now say, "Willa," and explain my daughter's name more easily if Mom was not nearby, cutting a swift and severe course across a lonely field.

Even into her seventies, Mom was a "walker." Dad went with the flow. In this way, he was able to bring Mom to places she'd never been. That fall, he even got her to agree to stay overnight in my house.

At a restaurant one night, Mom flatly denied that she was going anywhere when she used to storm out of our house.

"I never had doubts," she snapped.

I'd heard many versions of the past but never an all-out rewriting of history. Suddenly, I grew sweaty and tongue-tied.

"She's having doubts," Mom said, when Dad returned from the bathroom.

I kept my head down.

"It's probably just hormones," Mom observed when she saw a little precipitation around my eyes The next day, it was time for Mom to leave again.

Willa, Gwen, Henry and me in our family room, 2000

CHAPTER 19

Dial, Dial, Dial

2001

Like the training I once received, Ned's kids knew how to bring a phone to a dark bedroom.

"Yeah, he's right here," they'd say, walking the phone back through their ranch house.

Like them, I was always grateful when someone from beyond our dead had located my mom. Usually, it was my aunt. She was the only one who could pull Mom out of her darkness. But the calls from Aunt Gertrude only came about once a month and didn't last very long. By the time Mom had dragged herself to the little phone table in the living room, collapsed into the chair, and picked up the receiver, she was pretty spent. With great, heaving sobs, she'd fall upon the receiver. Then, she'd promise her sister to take better care of herself next time.

"Just that time of the month," she'd explain.

So, too, Ned would always make promises. He'd tell me he was planning to call his psychiatrist as soon as he got off the phone with me or when his wife came home from work.

But Ned got out of his bedroom more often than Mom. He made it to a few of his son's baseball games and his daughters' school events. One time, he even drove his wife and family up to my house for a visit.

As long as I never said words like "bipolar," "illness," "psychiatrist," or "hospital" around Ned, we had good visits. If I simply went along with the silence and pretended that Ned was like a travelling salesman, absent for large chunks of time every now and then, he'd continue taking my calls.

Still, I had pulled Ned out of his dark bedroom enough to know that "up" was not good when Dad put it in the handwritten, p.s. part of the weekly letter he always wrote: *As it happens, Ned seems to be in another up phase, but he has a saint for a wife and three wonderful kids and I'm sure time and love will sort everything out.*

I immediately started making calls.

By then, I'd learned a few things about Ed that were applicable to Ned. I'd learned, for example, that bipolar disorder was usually lethal, with one of the highest fatality rates of any known illness including cancer or heart disease.

Ned's psychiatrist, Dr. Caritas, was a younger man who took calls from me on Saturday nights. He also came recommended by a national bipolar network.

"Your brother is a really nice guy and he has a great family but he's frequently non-compliant," Dr. Caritas said one Saturday night.

This was a new word! Wasn't *not thinking he was ill* part of Ned's illness, in other words a symptom?

But Dr. Caritas was adamant. He was giving Ned one more chance. So, on that Saturday night in the spring of 2001, I set about trying to transport Ned from one part of my hometown to another via many long-distance calls.

I was getting good at these. Sometimes, I spent so much time on the phone that I forgot all about what was going on around me. On these occasions, Gwen and Willa could cover the kitchen in Bisquick before I realized what the little pancakes sprouting up all over their scalps were.

On the other hand, these long-distance calls reduced the number of times I left my four-bedroom Colonial for another attempted rescue mission at my dead end. For many years, I was hopping on a plane at the slightest hint of a storm. Trotting Henry, Gwen, or Willa in and out of all the locked parts of the hospital on my hip, I often felt more buoyant myself.

But instead of leaving my own family room that spring night, I picked up the phone to ask Dad to leave his. He'd been watching the ten p.m. news with Mom in their usual spot, but he was still game to put on his tennis shoes again.

"Ned is talking about Ed," I said.

This did the trick. In no time, Dad's car had arrived at the Barnes and Noble on the western edge of town, a few miles beyond the former Zeller, which had now been turned into a community college. I was pretty certain that Ned was here because I'd just held him on the pay phone there for about an hour. It seemed like a good place to try to keep Ned since there were already several sets of restraining orders against him in other parts of town.

That night, I heard Mom say, "Come on, Ned. Don't tell us you're going to make your old parents come out at midnight on a Saturday night for nothing,'" Apparently, she'd wasted no time in putting on her tennis shoes, as well.

At this point, Ned dropped the pay phone and I went to bed, feeling very warm next to Bart's hairy legs. With my new strategy, I'd been able to be in two places at the same time—my own intact Colonial and that old dark field of a parking lot, where Mom and Dad had just shone a light.

CHAPTER 20

Stop, Look, and Listen

Summer, 2001

Dad hadn't included the other piece of news in the postscript of that letter. He waited until I made my annual Fourth of July visit.

It was pretty busy around our dead end with Janet and her new toddler and Ned recently out of the hospital and Warren making more collect calls again. Fortunately, Dad and I found ourselves alone for a moment on a beautiful summer's day.

"So, how are you, Dad?" I asked.

I only asked this rhetorically because if anything were the matter, I would've known. "You take care of yourself. I'm taking care of mine," Dad always said rather emphatically.

Now, I waited for Dad's response. He was wearing an old cotton shirt, like the ones he'd always worn at Crooked Creek. The breeze was lifting his shirt as he stretched his arms out on a couple of nearby lawn chairs. But a moment's hesitation flashed across his face. Then, I heard a new kind of wind under our trees.

CHAPTER 21

Sweat It Out

August, 2001

Even after Dad told me about his cancer, I couldn't put down my project. I kept returning to that little space off my dining room, trying to find the word that had once made the wind stop.

Bell bottoms and hip huggers were in style again and it felt like we were going back in time. That's what I called it: "The Return of the Sixties." Otherwise, I didn't know what to make of the phone ringing again at the little phone table in my old living room.

I was surprised during my visit that year that I still knew the sequence of pauses that meant it was a collect call. But Mom's gushing tones were new. "Warren, don't say that. You know you always have a home to come back to," she yelled into the receiver. She was also jumping up from her swivel chair now to reach that faraway voice on the line.

Formerly, it was, "We're not running a nursing home!" or "You need to start taking responsibility for your own behaviour." But now, with Dad in the advanced stages of prostate cancer, Mom was inviting Warren back home for an indefinite stay.

After one of these calls, I overheard Dad say, "Well." He had begun spending a little more time in the corner of the couch . "Well" was his word for ordering things around our dead end. It was also a clue that he was getting ready to make another trip.

I feared that my Ed logic had begun to work too well. Mom said she wasn't about to lose another son and Dad claimed he wasn't feeling any side effects from the hormone replacement therapy. In fact, he insisted there was always something relaxing about a "getaway" — even to Kentucky in the middle of July.

But I beat my parents to Warren's apartment. I flew solo again. All of my kids were too big for schlepping around on my hip.

Warren was living in the border area of Ohio and Kentucky, where his dissertation advisor thought there might be some openings for adjunct history professors. There was a community college within walking distance, but Warren had yet to drop off his resume. There wouldn't have been an easy way to get ahold of him, anyway. As with other apartments, Warren didn't have a phone.

Still, he opened the door when I knocked. By then, I'd been able to locate a nurse practitioner within a fifty-mile radius who was willing to see Warren on a Saturday. Warren, in turn, was willing to try out that "little pill."

Sure enough, after a twenty-minute appointment, Warren walked out of her office with a bag full of Prozac samples. He began popping them on the way to dinner. After a few margaritas on the patio of Don Pablo's, he was feeling even better.

It was a very hot day and Warren and I had the whole patio to ourselves. Under staggering sun, we seemed to get closer. Warren didn't care if I asked all my questions again. Anything was fair game. He told me he knew "an awful lot" about the state of affairs under our trees before I was born.

He'd begun to have problems, he thought, in the middle grades, around the same time when Mom was finding religion.

She and Dad were closing the door to their room and having big arguments in those years. One time, Dad hid her shoes. Another time, Mom climbed out the bedroom window--perhaps after Dad hit her.

Either way, Mom kept going to the Christian Missionary Alliance Church across the field from us. Sometimes, she wouldn't come up from the basement for Warren's lunch. She was listening to the Moody Bible Hour. When Warren mentioned this to Dad, Mom pushed him out of his chair and called him a "snitch."

Warren was casual about all these details. He thought I knew most of them already.

I sort of did. I knew where Mom was going when she went down to our basement.

But I had wanted to go somewhere else with Warren.

Warren claimed he was happy now. He'd let go of a lot of things that had once had a hold on him—sex, pot, foreign films. He said he was even grateful for the way his marijuana plants had let him down. At one time, they were the only things keeping him alive. Now, he claimed he was "free."

This was always Mom's word. But it wasn't the word I was looking for. I was still for "A Hard Day's Night."

CHAPTER 22

Eat Fish

Late Fall, 2001

When Warren ran out of Prozac, he found himself in some rough places. Even the liquor store outside his apartment wasn't very helpful. By 9/11, he was turning yellow but he had some doubts about getting back in Mom and Dad's car. They wanted to rescue him again that day.

Back at our dead end, Warren agreed to undergo treatment for alcohol and chemical addiction. Unfortunately, after successful completion of the program Warren still wasn't exactly well. Neither neuroscientists, cardiac specialists, nor liver doctors knew what to make of the speech and bowel difficulties that had begun to plague Warren as soon as he took up residence in his old bedroom. Nevertheless, Dad didn't give up. He wanted to be "useful." So, he began pulling Warren out of bed and into the shower on a regular basis.

Warren has complained the car is driving on rims, there is a peculiar odor in the house, thinks all doors are locked, etc. The doctor doubled the mood elevator but that will take a couple weeks to kick in. He has stayed in AA program. He is extremely critical of everything. Mom went with him today to her dentist to get his teeth straightened out. The head may be more difficult. Time will tell. We are fine. We see some humor in all this. Warren reminds us of things to do. He does dishes and small jobs if you stand over him—like you have to do with a kid. I'm beginning to think he had some kind of stroke.

(letter from Dad, October 2001)

It's a slippery slope, this abrupt change of personality in Sir Warren George. Your father has a wonderful upbeat attitude about it and sings his favorite songs when he comes home from the Y to get Warren up to take to the office. Today W. bounded down the stairs rarin' to go but loud and vocal while enjoying his grapefruit, toast, and coffee.

(letter from Mom, October 2001)

Thankfully, when Thanksgiving rolled around, Bart offered to grill the turkey. For a change, Dad took him up on it.

As a result, I was able to give Mom and Dad a little respite care at their favorite bed and breakfast across town.

"Oh, my god," Warren said upon entering my house.

He had walked up to my door on his own as Mom and Dad backed out of my driveway. He was not cheered at the sight of toys on the floor of my family room. Nor did he seem to notice that I had cleared my buffet and done some vacuuming, besides. Instead, he shuffled through the house toward the guest bedroom, fixing his gaze on a stick of butter sitting out in the kitchen.

I was surprised by these reactions from an ex-hippie. I was even more surprised the next day when Warren wanted me to warm up the cappuccino Bart had made for him. It was two p.m. and Warren was still in Bart's pajamas. For some reason, Mom had packed nothing but tee-shirts and underwear in his little suitcase. Bart's bottoms were dangerously long and falling all about Warren but he managed to make it down the stairs.

Willa was still a toddler and when Warren came down the stairs she was right there to greet him. This obstructed Warren's passage. Instead of saying anything, though, Warren merely looked somewhere else until she moved. At that age, Willa seemed to understand Warren's form of communication.

I was less fluent. I tried to wield Dad's old spatula in the kitchen. Meanwhile, Warren watched everything I did and touched.

"Wh-----arrrrr----time is it?" he asked.

I pointed to the clock and explained that if we were going to Gwen's kindergarten performance at three he'd need to get dressed soon. He asked for more clarification. Then, h went back upstairs.

Later, I wondered how any of us could have imagined squeezing Warren into one of the tiny chairs set up in Gwen's classroom for the class performance of *Chickachickaboomboom*.

Still, this was the plan we'd discussed. Dad said it was too bad that Warren couldn't make it. He was eager to look in on him. He knew I'd hidden all the booze in our house, but he didn't like the idea of Warren being left alone.

Even Gwen understood the situation. At six, she could see that her uncle was having trouble with speech, continence, and perception. She knew that being pulled into a tiny chair in the center of a crowded room would not make Warren feel better. So, she wasn't disappointed that Warren couldn't make it. Instinctively, she seemed to know that not everyone from my dead end would fit into her classroom.

Indeed, I was beginning to get sweaty under all those fluorescent lights. They were so bright that I could see Mom looking very alert in her multiple layers. She called these scarves, tee-shirts, sweatshirts, and hairbands "gifts." According to her, Ed had dropped them for her along her walks. Even Dad, for once, looked a little out-of-place. He was waiting to get back to Warren with his tan overcoat draped over his arm.

With her quiet, knowing smile, Gwen grabbed my hand. She knew we were never going to be the clan with the video camera or the ones to linger at the punch bowl. Still, she wanted me there. Seizing the opportunity, she insisted on introducing me to her teacher and showing me all her artwork. She wouldn't let me use Willa as an excuse for another quick exit.

When we got home, Warren was still in bed. But he came down to the family room when Bart got back from work. By then, Warren had a long list of concerns, complaints, and anxieties about the proposed dinner plan.

"That's impossible!" Warren wailed in response to Henry's request for a little pre-dinner scrimmage with his grandfather.

"Keep counting," Dad said to Henry. "I'll bet your uncle reaches 100 negative statements soon."

"That's fifty-one," Henry said when Warren complained again. As Warren began to look more and more agitated, I tried to make certain facial gestures toward Henry.

Bart later told me that my dad was only trying to make Warren's disorder less scary for Henry, though. He'd done the same with me. All those years on our dead end, he'd had someone who still needed French toast amidst the storms.

That night, we eventually made it to the fish restaurant Dad wanted to try because he'd read an article about the positive effects of fish oils on the brain. It was late when Mom finally finished her salad. Before she could finish her entree, Bart had long since taken the kids home.

In their wake, Dad became more expansive. He was turning eighty that year and he reflected on how happy he'd been in this latter phase of his life. He'd recently read some old, suggestive letters Mom had written to him at sea.

"I didn't want him to go looking for women in other ports," she piped up before bowing over her plate again.

Dad just beamed. He claimed he'd finally gotten "his old Wilma" back.

As Dad explained that night, "Time and Love" were the keys to everything: a good marriage, a happy life, rewarding family relationships. As if in demonstration, he leaned back in the booth and watched Mom work on her food.

Mom didn't look up from her plate. Seeing this, I began my old three-part harmony project and made several observations about Mom's "free" spirit. Warren struck a different note. He began to warn about the dangers of the religious right. For some reason, he didn't have any problem pronouncing these syllables.

Mom promptly launched into her old, soulful "walk with God" soliloquy. With her face squeezed into an ecstatic pout, she announced that she wouldn't give up Christ for the world!

By this point, Dad began looking for the check and we split along gender lines leaving the restaurant. Dad and Warren were in front and Mom and me were a few steps behind but not out of earshot when she started going back into the past and how she and Dad hadn't known anything as young parents and how they'd do *everything* differently now.

By the time we got to the car, Warren was stamping his feet. It was a damp night and he was trying to stay warm.

"Best parents in the universe!" he exclaimed before climbing back in my car. Then, he looked Mom and Dad straight in the eye and flashed one of his old smiles.

This meant that Dad had been right all along. There was something very healing about fish.

CHAPTER 23

Let it Be

May, 2002

It must've been in between my call and the call Dad made to his brother that he found the energy to perform his old trick. Maybe Dad wanted to call his brother in peace. Maybe he knew it would be one of the last times they talked. Maybe he didn't want his brother to worry about him. Or maybe Dad just wanted to be heard.

To be sure, there had been a lot of background noise around our dead end that spring. "Whaaa . . . er . . . hey . . ." Warren would say for almost any situation, including whenever Dad picked up the phone. Though Dad had devoted himself to Warren throughout the fall and winter, it wasn't clear by late April that all the navy bean soup and cozy fires were working. With the slightest disruption, Warren could get pretty loud.

So, Dad did his old bait and switch that night. Would Warren be so kind as to get him a beer from the six-pack he'd been hiding in the garage? Dad wasn't moving very fast then.

He had to calculate the time it would take Warren to go and come back carefully. The cancer was now in his bones.

And Warren fell for the trick. As soon as Dad mentioned "beer," Warren pulled himself out of his corner of the couch and stepped out the front door. Maybe Warren was thinking about the fact that Mom was at church. Maybe he thought about all those old times when he and Dad had kept each other company. Maybe he thought they could get back to that place tonight.

Whatever it was, Warren went. Dad didn't waste any time. He got up from the little phone table in the living room and quickly chainlocked *both* doors. Even if this meant that Dad had effectively barricaded himself within his own house, it also meant he could pick up the phone and make his last call to his brother in peace.

But Warren knew how to make himself heard. No matter how far away he went, he'd always made it back. Once again, he was pounding at the front door.

This time, the neighbors came to our rescue. Perhaps they'd been observing Dad's decreasing mobility that spring. They saw, perhaps, that he wouldn't be able to load his own ambulance anymore. They maybe heard what we'd been trying to say all those years. They called for help.

As usual, a squad car came. The police officers managed to get Warren down on the ground and into handcuffs, but he was still making a lot of noise when Mom strolled back across the field from church.

"I don't have any sympathy for you," she proudly reported herself as having said to Warren that night. She acted as if she'd finally found her vocal cords, too.

All was quiet, then, by the time I flew down the next weekend. I wasn't even sure why I'd come. It was Bart's idea again. He said I needed to *see* my dad. Otherwise, I might miss something.

All I could see when I arrived, though, was that Dad was going up and down the stairs to his office just like everyone had reported. Even if his appetite was a little diminished, he could still sip some tomato soup while Ned and I caught up over lunch at a downtown cafe. Then, he was eager to finish an appraisal back at his office. He also took notes on all the clinical trials I'd found out about.

So, I tended to Mom and visited Warren in the hospital that weekend. I left Dad to his swims at the Y and news shows in the rec room.

It was a little damp out there that Saturday afternoon. Dad was sitting alone in Warren's old chair. He said he'd been listening to one of the Beatles CDs he'd bought for Warren that winter, thinking it would cheer Warren up. When they built the rec room, Dad observed, he thought it would be a great room for a person to convalesce.

"That's probably what you'll be doing this year," I said, trying for Dad's old sinsong.

"May-be," Dad replied.

No one had built a fire but Dad had one of Mom's afghans draped loosely around his shoulders. It looked like a cape as Dad leaned his head close to the boom box. He was listening to "A Day in the Life" and I waited for his old "isn't this pleasant?" smile. He just listened and later said he was happy that he now had time to hear all the words.

As on so many other occasions, I still had a few questions for Dad.

"What about Mom?" I asked, looking for that word again.

Dad knew what subject I was back on. He took a breath before saying, "She's str-ong."

The word I was looking for would've had more syllables, I thought. This one had only two, like many of the other words Dad often used to describe the complicated nature of life under our trees. "Time and Love" were some others.

So, I asked my question a different way. How, again, did the stock market crash of 1929 and subsequent Great Depression explain our dead end?

"Unless that's just what they called it," Dad said before getting up and walking out to the kitchen to heat up a little soup for himself.

He'd never hinted at any such theory before. He'd never lumped Mom's family together, either. Still, he'd slipped a few hints into some of his letters to me over the years. One of these was a copy of a family chronology in Grandmother Bueckle's handwriting. I'd pinned it up on my bulletin board in the study and stared at it many times when the sentences wouldn't come. I liked looking at the handwriting of the grandmother I'd only visited once or twice when Mom was still driving.

Had I been a better student of history those dates might've caught my eye. They told the story that Dad had perhaps been trying to tell me all along in his characteristic "think for yourself, Juney" shorthand. It was not about The Great Depression, then.

Watching Dad pull himself out of Warren's old chair that weekend, I realized that even Dad might have been lonely around our dead end. He'd always tried to make enough space for everyone, but with the never-ending nature of our wind, there was never going to be a table where we could all fit. Often, Dad had been in the background, making sure everyone else got fed.

A few months earlier, he had stayed overnight at my house for an out-of-town funeral. It was late February but he was moving easily then, jumping up from my couch to toss a few footballs to Henry in the snow. I played some Don McLean on the stereo and Dad jumped up again. Like Ned once running through the house at the sound of *"Long, long time ago,"* Dad was out in the middle of my family room, looking for a partner with *"Did you write the book of love?"* Gwen came running, followed shortly by Willa. Soon, Dad was twirling both granddaughters on either arm, cutting the rug with that old shoe-licking, double-time step I'd seen on Ed at Walt and Toni's wedding.

I stayed on the sidelines. I couldn't see what was disappearing *fast*.

Even the oncologist couldn't necessarily *see* Dad at his last appointment. This was a day a few days after I flew home when Dad asked Ned for a ride. Dad also asked the oncologist if he could admit himself into the hospital. The oncologist said, "Okay."

So, Mom walked Dad across the street and left him in what she called a "suite." He was in good spirits and getting ready for radiation treatments the next morning. "Any chest pain?" they had asked in admissions.

In the middle of the night, during that hour when Dad used to steer very large ships through icy waters, he suffered a massive heart attack. The cardiologist who had been on call said it had been "very difficult" to bring him back. Still, Dad was almost whistling when I arrived the next day.

"Keep swimming, Dad," I said about the little blowing sounds he was making with his mouth.

"Is that painkiller coming soon?" he wondered.

I had not rushed to the hospital. I had taken my time, stopping by Dad's old church, chatting with the minister, making visits to Warren and calls to Ned, Janet and Walt.

Mom, too, had walked down to the hospital at a leisurely pace. She was a little breathless when she reached Dad in the intensive care unit. She'd seen him in a coffin in a horrible dream, she explained. She was so relieved to find him still here.

I held Dad's hand as long as I could, but I kept sweating out the orange-striped tee-shirt I'd worn. I'd worn it thinking of that beach long ago where Dad had tried to bring us. But I had to keep running to the bathroom to wipe down my armpits. As I result, I wasn't there when Dad began asking rather anxiously, "Where's Wilma and June?"

I happened to be in the cafeteria. I'd already spent a good half hour there watching Mom work through her all-you-can-eat salad.

"What's your hurry?" she asked at one of the sunny tables.

She had just caught her breath, she said, and she wanted to finish her plate. With every bite, she made sundry observations about the sunlight, the food, and the smiling people around the room. At one point, she glanced outside. There was Warren in the smoker's courtyard. He'd been brought out with a group from his unit. When he saw Mom through the glass, he flashed a huge smile. Mom was floored. He hadn't smiled like that for years, she observed.

Things were quiet when we arrived back up on Dad's floor. A little while earlier, Dad had waved everyone out of the room with a song. We all got a big kick out of that. *"Goodnight, ladies,"* he'd sung. With that, it wasn't long before Dad took his last breath and made one more dive into the deep.

CHAPTER 24

Plant Before The Danger of Frost

Summer, 2002

At ten years of age, Henry did not get the joke as I tried to tell it. I was explaining how I'd brought Warren down in the elevator after Dad died. A little circle of us had formed around Dad's still warm chest and Walt was offering some remarks. Soon, another sound could be heard and Walt's jaw dropped.

"Hey, that's 'The Chambered Nautilus'!" Walt exclaimed, pointing to Warren in the corner. By then, Warren had moved closer to Dad. I could see tears dropping from his eyes onto Dad's chest. Meanwhile, not one muscle on Warren's face moved.

"I guess," Henry said, exhaling with a weary sigh. "But Mom, it's not funny. You should feel sorry for your brother. He can't help it."

This implied I could.

Henry was one of the few to cry at Dad's funeral. Even though he was much too short to reach the microphone, he had walked up to the podium.

"I just played football with Grandpa!" he stammered before finding his way back to Bart, who was also crying.

Even though the whole town came out, I had barely remembered to order casket flowers. I had to be prompted by Walt's wife, Toni. After the graveside services were over, I was right back on the phone again. Warren was ready to be released from the hospital. Walt wondered where he should go. I claimed there was plenty of extra space in my Colonial.

When Bart caught wind of this, his face darkened. In fact, it seemed like his face might've been darkening for some time, only I hadn't noticed.

That was when Bart made it clear that I'd have to find a different co-captain if I insisted on turning our four-bedroom Colonial into another dead end. Indeed, the state of things around our house could not continue, he implied. In a word, I needed *help*.

Fortunately, I found a very good therapist who quickly saw what was missing under all my trees. I'd known this all along. I'd seen all the pairs of dark eyes. I'd seen them for so long I hadn't been able to see my own.

Only with Dad's death could I see the circle and myself as a part of it. That was when I began to realize what I'd been asking Dad all that time. I also saw what he'd been trying to tell me. Indeed, there really hadn't been anything so terribly wrong with my dead end when I considered the alternatives.

I couldn't see what I'd gone without, though. As long as I had my French-toast maker beside me, I felt solid. Even Dad may have wanted more. He'd always talked about "serving his fellow man." I worried that he wanted to leave us. Now, I wondered if he'd gathered us into the living room that night in order to bring us into a place where we could be *seen* and where he could be seen *with* us.

My therapist had asked, "So, you're a mom who takes her kids to the park?" like a doctor in a movie who had suddenly stumbled across a very interesting symptom.

"Yeah," I shrugged.

"Good. That's very good," she said, suggesting that my prognosis wasn't terminal.

I nodded gratefully, in the same way I'd nodded at all the mothers who offered to push my kids on the swings and all the teachers and neighbors who had delighted in my children's mismatched socks and easy smiles, calling them "free spirits."

All of these freelance caregivers seemed to have time to stop and notice my kids. They didn't need to get to the bottom of the past in order to navigate the present. Somehow, they could step out of their own house on a gorgeous spring day without wondering whether they or their loved ones were headed toward the garage

Knowing what I did about wind, though, I wondered where everyone else put their wind. How did they make sure it didn't blow everything around?

With cancer in his bones and his heart giving out, Dad had spent his last year firing off footballs to Henry, taking Gwen to buy her first dress, teaching Willa how to swim, writing poems to Mom about the night they met, completing Walt's legal work, babysitting for Janet, building fires for Warren, and keeping Ned at work on appraisals whenever possible. How did he make so many things grow straight and tall even under the weight of all our trees?

*The sea had jeeringly kept his finite body up, but drowned
the infinite of his soul.*

"THE CASTAWAY," MOBY DICK

From left: Janet, Walt, Warren, Mom, Ned, and June at Dad's funeral on May 7, 2002

CHAPTER 25

Spell It Out

2003

When the bank closed Dad's office a year after his death, Ned began cancelling his psychiatric appointments. Soon, his wife, Ruth, was threatening divorce. As if protecting him from the next blow, Ruth had embraced Ned from behind at Dad's funeral, stayed up all night with him on many occasions, brought him fresh jeans every time he was admitted into the hospital, and stored all his albums.

Still, Ned was nonchalant. He ripped up the prescription Ruth begged him to take and walked away from his marriage, declaring, "I feel more fit than I have in a long time." Soon, he was under a restraining order. Then, he wasn't going anywhere.

In a one-bedroom apartment a block or two from his three-bedroom ranch, he moved into a corner that summer. By October, Janet was leaving food at the door and Mom was trying to talk him into some fresh air whenever she went out for a walk. Ned wouldn't budge.

Over the phone, he made another deal with me, though. He promised he would go to his psychiatrist within 24 hours if I wouldn't call the Emergency Response Service.

Later, Henry said, "Next time, Mom, don't tell Uncle Ned you're calling ERS. Just call them."

Apparently, my threat lit such a fire under Ned that, instead of going to his doctor, he drove straight out of town the next morning until he found a pick-up truck in the opposite lane to run into. Mom didn't think Ned was trying to commit suicide, though. She thought he'd just been hungry for a roast beef sandwich at an apple orchard we used to go to outside of town.

Warren knew otherwise. "What do you do with someone who can't eat, who's probably hearing voices, who has all sorts of fears of people coming to his apartment? You threaten them with ERS!?" he yelled at me over the phone from his seniors apartment. This was a place the social worker from the nearby nursing home found for him. I'd found the nursing home off a downtown highway in Minneapolis. It was the only place that had been willing to take Warren upon his discharge from the hospital in our hometown without an in-take interview. And Walt's wife, Toni, volunteered to provide transportation. She didn't even have any of my Dad's old trouble getting Warren into the car. She simply turned on an old rock-n-roll station and let him smoke to his heart's content.

Once Warren was in my neck of the woods, I got rather good at this transportation technique myself. Over the course of that year after Dad's death, I took Warren to many different appointments and had a few good conversations over lunch at McDonald's.

But now I reverted straight back to standard procedure at my dead end.

"Let's see how would you have handled it!" I shouted into the receiver. Before Warren could hang up, I also added that he should never have been allowed out of the locked-up psychiatric units he'd been in.

Of course, my kids heard all of this. They were in the family room on the couch with Bart. They'd come close to losing another uncle and were sobbing as I slammed down the receiver. But I didn't go to them. Instead, I picked up the phone again and began making plans to fly back to my hometown. If I left quickly emough, I could miss out on all the family activities for Halloween.

Of course, there really wasn't too much of a hurry with Ned. He didn't wake up from his coma until a few weeks later. Even if I didn't stay by his bedside all that time, I was there when he did resurface, sputtering and leaking as never before.

"Ned," I said, as he sobbed and cried, "it wasn't our house, it wasn't our trees, it wasn't Mom, it wasn't even a monster. It was only mental illness. That's all."

Finally, I seemed to have found the word. I was crying now, too, and it looked like Ned and I weren't too far from our old kitchen table. With any luck, we'd be able to get everyone else back there, too.

But Mom warned me about becoming too "outspoken." She wouldn't participate in the family therapy I tried to orchestrate. She wouldn't even come to my house that winter after Ned got out of his rehabilitation center and the two of them decided on a spur-of-the-moment trip. They were in good spirits when I picked them up at the Hubert Humphrey Terminal.

Ned seemed to have bounced back from his suicide attempt no worse for wear. He took me up on my offer of a guest room while Bart was travelling overseas. Mom chose to keep Warren company in his seniors apartment.

Unfortunately, the unevenness and slight limp from Ned's head injury became more pronounced when he refused to take his medications at my house. We were having a "discussion" in my living room that night. After overhearing a little of it, Henry asked me quietly in the kitchen, "Mom, why do you argue with Uncle Ned? Can't you see he has a head injury?"

"Because Henry," I insisted, "Uncle Ned is now claiming he doesn't have bipolar disorder!"

At this, Henry grew wide-eyed and walked into the living room.

"Uncle Ned, what if your kids get bipolar disorder?" Henry asked. "Wouldn't you want to tell them about your experience to help them?"

On this note, Ned stood up very straight and exclaimed, "What if the world blows up?" Then, he stormed out of my living room to sit in the dark of my family room.

Needless to say, it wasn't long before Mom and Ned flew back to our dead end. All that spring and summer, they were quite a pair with Mom gladly leaping out of her swivel chair whenever Ned showed up in a taxi from whatever apartment or motel Walt and Janet tried to establish him in. In the midst of all that activity, Mom couldn't be bothered with how much money Ned was spending or where he was going after-hours.

"Ned's an adult now," she said to me.

"Then, why does he want to move into his old bedroom?" I asked.

After Mom hung up on me, Henry said, "Mom, you shouldn't get mad at Grandma. She can't help it, either."

Once again, this implied I could.

"She's lonely," Henry explained.

But it wasn't long before Mom was even lonelier. That was the May night, roughly two years after Dad's death, when Ned began throwing the furniture from the room he'd just moved into down the stairs. Now, Ned effectively barricaded himself so well that Mom felt the need for escape. In the middle of the night, she slipped out the back door in her nightgown and went looking for a pay phone.

This was because the phone at the little phone table in the living room where Mom never answered it wasn't there. Walt had come over earlier that day and, with Mom's permission, taken it away because Ned had been using it to jam the switchboard at his law office.

Even though the pay phone three blocks up the street was broken and there was no sign of a police car anywhere near our dead end that night, Mom was resourceful. Using her old strategies, she walked around in the dark for several hours until she saw a light. It was the little ranch house across from our dead end. Now, for the first time in her life, Mom walked up to that door and yelled, "Help!"

CHAPTER 26

Let It All Hang Out

2004

At age eight, Gwen was dark-haired and high-cheeked like Mom had been with a spirited step to match. Even though Gwen was very independent and what my mom called "stubborn," Gwen never liked to be far from me. In addition, she'd never been willing to watch as much PBS as Henry. Instead, she'd spent a lot of her preschool years in my study, watching me go back under all my old trees.

Gwen was sitting on my lap, then, when Mom said, "Ooo, that looks good," licking her lips with a hungry smile across from us. As a grandmother, she often kept her distance. But Willa and Gwen didn't take this as a rejection. They ran to the old kitchen table whenever Mom pulled out the ice cream with Cocoa Puffs for breakfast.

On this visit, I had asked Mom to tell Gwen and Willa about her old boarding school days. I wanted my daughters to know more about "the walker," "the rebel," "the free spirit."

So, as Mom sat in a lawn chair, looking like Katherine Hepburn in *African Queen,* I gave my daughters a squeeze. I knew which story Mom was going to tell. It was the one about arriving at her first boarding school, a large house in upstate New York that two sisters ran.

Mom had been the new kid on the block, she explained to Gwen and Willa, flashing her sneaky, licorice smile. There was another girl in the center, who was "A-OK," as Mom put it.

"So, I jumped her," Mom stated.

"Jumped her?" Gwen asked, alarmed.

"Yes, you know. Haven't you ever jumped someone?"

Gwen shook her head, dismayed at the image of her grandmother as a bully. I was a little confused, too. I only remembered Mom as the victim in these stories.

Mom continued, reciting the details in the same cadence I'd heard many times. As always, Mom's voice turned into a skipping sort of laugh at the point in the story where she had the girl "pinned."

I'd never been able to picture this.

"You know how you get your knees up over the chest and pin their elbows to the ground," Mom explained.

I'd always seen Mom the other way around--as pinned, not pinning.

"I had her down," Mom continued, "but the other girls began clapping and cheering for her. Just then my barrette popped and she flipped me."

I'd forgotten that part, too.

Gwen's big, brown eyes grew sad.

"That was the night when I had what you'd call a kind of crisis in my bunk," Mom said.

"I felt so lonely I couldn't breathe. I didn't know how to pray, but I called out to my Heavenly Father. That calmed me," Mom concluded. She was swinging her leg and flashing her old tricky smile again.

So, the story wasn't funny after all. I wanted to cry. So did Gwen and Willa. Mom only kept nodding her head with an adamant upswing.

She'd attended a grief group for awhile after Dad's death but when they said she couldn't stay in it forever she quit going. And whenever she came up north, she insisted on staying in Warren's apartment. She was always too out of breath to come to my house a few miles away.

If I wanted to see her, I had to find her. She liked walking around the lakes with Warren. His hips were tentative and they walked very slowly, but they looked like a pair. Warren tended to watch his step as gazed off toward the horizon.

I couldn't understand why Mom wouldn't come over for even a meal. I promised her Bart would do all the cooking. Still, she said, "Nothin' doin'," or, "I don't want anyone going to all that rigmarole on my behalf!"

If I made a very flexible plan, she was happy to meet me at playgrounds and the hot tub at the YWCA pool. In the dressing rooms afterwards, she'd take long, hot showers. She walked around naked with my daughters.

"I'm really frustrated with you right now, Mom," I blurted out after one of these visits. She couldn't fathom why. Jiggling her head, she began to look at the door handle to see if there was an easy way out,

"You were here for two weeks," I said.

Now she was sucking in her breath.

"I knew I should've gotten a taxi," she muttered.

Because she hadn't, she had to put up with me for a whole hour before her train came. In those chairs in the waiting lounge, I called her out on every single one of her weather or hayfever-related excuses for never stepping foot in my house and only caring to see her grandkids when I brought them to her.

Finally, she admitted the truth: she was more comfortable in Warren's one-bedroom. She said it was cozy.

I understood that. Sometimes, I felt the same way about my study.

So, when I walked Mom out to the tracks, we were a little closer. She let me walk her all the way into the car. Even then, she didn't let go of my hand. Finally, peering down from a dark stairwell, she said, "You know I'd be lost without you."

Now I knew what Dad meant. Once I'd seen that fierce, frightened face, there was no way to let go.

Me and Mom on the beach, circa 1973

CHAPTER 27

Add Parts

October, 2005

"Half a person," Mom said with no apparent reference one night during a visit I'd made for her eightieth birthday in January. I noticed she'd been putting up more family photos. She claimed that on many days she kissed the old faces behind the glass. This meant she made it all the way out to the living room.

She'd had ample time to think, she said, and she'd now decided that our family was divided into "whole" and "half-people." She said this in the rec room one night as I was beginning to doze off. She was still very alert in the blinking light of the television.

"How can you tell?" I asked, pretending I hadn't seen these divisions, too.

"You can see it in the way they enter a room," Mom said. "Whole people don't need to be coaxed or nudged into the world. But half-people have to be brought along. Like Dad always saying, 'Come on, Wilma.'"

I realized, though, that Dad had also frequently let Mom stay in bed. After a certain point, he didn't make many demands. He had a large family by then. Perhaps he didn't want to risk it. Six kids with a mother in the back bedroom is better than six kids with no mother at all, or one who, like Mom's own, was "away."

Allowing Mom to stay in bed also made it possible for the rest of us to come and go more freely through grade school, high school, and college. As long as Mom was given "a wide berth," she didn't become disruptive or the sort of threat that some of my brothers later became known for around our local courthouse, office buildings, and school grounds. Nevertheless, none of these strategies had kept our wind confined.

"How can you tell whether whole people only look whole to others?" I asked as a follow-up.

Mom clapped her hands in delight at this irony, but I was tired by then. I wouldn't stay up all night and keep her company in the dark. I was beginning to see everything a little too clearly under our bare branches. I saw the two of us, both still incomplete and alone despite all of Dad's care and French toast. I couldn't keep listening as Mom went back over her childhood again. She wanted to show me how she'd somehow become more "ma-toor" through family collapse, boarding school, and a kind of indifference on the part of all the teachers, ministers, and care professionals she'd ever encountered.

All I said was, "What if everyone secretly feels like a half-person?" without bothering to explain who I meant.

CHAPTER 28

Bring On the Berries

October, 2005

Before long, Mom and Ned were on separate floors of
the hospital just like Dad and Warren a few years earlier.
Apparently, we had plenty of pairs who had needed more care
than our dead end could provide.

"Ooo, that feels good!" Mom exclaimed after every hug and
touch. She was more visible now that her stomach was swelled
up with cancer. Fortunately, Walt had stopped by that day
when she didn't answer her phone. Otherwise, she might never
have made it out of her bed.

With widespread cancer and a prescription for Prozac, she
was reaching out to kiss everyone and learning all the names
of the nurses. She even began to make plans for her life. She no
longer drooped at the sight of an active grandkid but greeted
everyone by name, pronouncing each and every letter..

Finally, she looked like that mother who had once pulled me
fast and thrillingly on a sled. She was graceful yet firm, politely

excusing her old minister and his wife after they spent a few hours trying to "pray her into heaven."

Indeed, now that Mom was about to die she was no longer waiting for The Second Coming. She claimed she'd only been trying to escape herself with Billy Graham.

"I'd always tried to be such a good girl and not make trouble for anyone," she finally explained, diagnosing herself with a "lifelong inferiority complex."

I didn't search for a better word. I only cried and told her she was a "trouper." When she lost her voice and wrote "too much pollen" in her old, lilting cursive on a notepad, I cleared all the flowers out of her room.

With her last breaths, Mom called Warren and told him that she understood why he couldn't come to her funeral, helped Walt with all the legal work, let Janet wash her hair, and indulged me in a few verses of "Shuffle Off to Buffalo." At the very end, she even tracked Ned down somewhere out there in the night. Ever since she'd told him he couldn't move back in the bedroom he'd taken apart, he'd been bouncing from hospital to jail to bar. But he made it into the hospital just in time. Once Mom knew Ned was safe and secure a few floors above her, she slipped into a coma herself.

As with Dad, we somewhat scattered when Mom's end came. I was back in Mom's favorite spot, the cafeteria, having breakfast with Walt and Toni. When Janet came running to find us, Mom took a cue from Dad dropped into the deep alone.

The next day, the minister of the Southside Rescue Mission asked the little congregation to light a candle for "Sister Wheel-ma." A breast cancer survivor, herself, she called Mom a survivor, too.

By then, I'd found out a little more about "the walker." By taking Mom's route through town that Sunday, I learned about where my mother was going when she headed out into the unprotected spaces of a typical Midwestern city where she was considered "different." Balancing along busy thoroughfares with steep gulleys on either side, Mom often avoided the broad sidewalks of middle-class neighborhoods for the "shortcuts."

She claimed these stretches through poorer areas with chain-link fencing and guard dogs were "family" neighborhoods.

But I hadn't always seen where my mother went when she left our dead end. I only saw she was gone.

Gwen, on the other hand, seemed to know more about her grandmother for having spent so little time with her. At the funeral, she described the way in which her grandmother had dashed out of the house and over to the Amish sisters' backyard on summer mornings. Then, before anyone else had a chance, she bought up all their berries. Delivering the flat back to our dead end, she laid it out on a little picnic table in the front yard for all the grandkids to "gobble up."

On the second day; a sail drew near, nearer, and picked me
up at last. It was the devious-cruising Rachel, that
in her retracing search after her missing children,
only found another orphan.

HERMAN MELVILLE
"EPILOGUE," *MOBY DICK*

Front to back: Willa, Henry, and Gwen by a heat register, 2000

CHAPTER 29

Hear Your Own Echo

Spring, 2006

By the time I could finally hear the fullness of my children's voices, they seemed to have begun talking about absence. Apparently, they'd been drifting toward heat registers for a number of years. I'd only come far enough on that Saturday in 2006 to locate them.

They'd spread themselves throughout the house that morning as if they were trying to fill it completely. With Bart travelling again, there was no one in the kitchen. Willa had taken up a spot in the middle of the house, anyway. This way, she had to be stepped over by anyone trying to go from one end to the other.

"Wait, Mom has *four* brothers?" she said that Saturday morning, wearing last night's clothes. At six years of age, she was often left to put her own thoughts together, and she frequently used this heat vent to do it. With light hair and a pair of beauty moles above her lip, her face would take on a dreamy look like Marilyn Monroe as she stared at the blank wall ahead of her.

"Figure it out, Willa!" Gwen fired back from a living room chair, where she'd been hanging upside down and waiting for some action that morning.

Now, Willa had to begin counting agian.

"There's Uncle Walt, Uncle Ned, Uncle Warren. Who else?" Willa asked.

"Uncle Ed," Henry answered without missing a beat.

He was looking around in the refrigerator, trying to see if something fresh had yet arrived.

"Uncle Ed?" Willa repeated, scrunching up her face at the sound of this foreign country.

"You know, the guy Mom's writing her book about," Gwen stated in a matter-of-fact tone. She'd obviously practiced this tone--probably whenever her friends and their parents asked, "Where's your mom?"

"Where is Uncle Ed, then?" Willa wondered, looking around.

"Ed died," Henry said, still ready with perfectly timed and clearly stated answers.

"He died a long time ago," Gwen added, trying to sound like Henry.

"Ed is dead?" Willa asked again, growing sad and confused.

"You didn't know about Edward?" demanded Henry, getting tired of another fruitless search in the fridge.

"Ed-ward?" Willa repeated as if this was yet another new country.

"Ed is short for Edward, silly!" Gwen yelled.

"Oh," Willa answered.

By this time, Henry had discovered a hidden bag of oranges in a far corner of a lower shelf. Handpicked from his grandparents in Florida, Henry's find had somehow gone undetected by everyone else in the house including me. If I'd found it, chances were, I'd find a way like Mom to "get rid of it." She didn't like any excess.

Seizing upon this new food, Henry cast about, trying to decide how best to turn it into long-lasting nourishment. Finally, he decided on squeezing the oranges. To avoid any pulp getting stuck in his braces, though, he needed to squeeze them very carefully. He needed a juice strainer, bowl, and clean glass, none of which was readily available in a kitchen with all the disorder and dirty dishes of a mother who was "away."

Nevertheless, Henry persevered and assembled what he needed without calling for help. He'd learned early on that it was much easier to work alone in the kitchen than to walk all the way back to my study and ask for assistance. Even if I wasn't as far away on this Saturday as I'd been on some others, he decided not to involve me. Instead, he made his way to the one spot of clear space and stood at the sink with a hopefulness like Dad's.

Now, Gwen and Willa began to slide in closer. Just like another older brother I knew, Henry was providing lights, camera, and action on this Saturday morning. In search of just such a gathering, Gwen and Willa brought chairs, pillows, bowls, and spoons to the spot Henry had staked out. They wanted to start up a juice factory with him.

But Henry held fast to the precious oranges he'd found. He'd been looking forward to his little burst of sensory stimulation. Now, he wanted to enjoy the fruits of his labor in peace and quiet, just as I had always done with my French toast. Finishing out the conversation, he turned around from the sink and held up his fresh-squeezed juice like a trophy.

"Don't you know that I'm named after Ed, Willa?" he asked.

"Huh?" Willa asked, thoroughly confused.

"You don't know my middle name!" Henry said.

Willa tried out a few before giving up.

"It's Mom's younger brother," Gwen offered as a hint.

"**Older**," Henry corrected. He was getting ready to leave the kitchen, but before he did he wanted to get some things straight. So, he said, "Henry Edward. He said it so it sounded right. Then, he picked up his glass of juice. "Who's teaching you two history?" he asked on the way out.

It was about as cross as Henry ever got about all the shortages and gaps around our house. He didn't mind doing his own wash or wearing hand-me-downs or arranging his own hockey rides or being the only one whose mom wasn't waiting in the lobby at the orthodontist's office. He even tucked everyone in at night with a personal, "I love you."

But he was getting tired of making his own breakfast on Saturday mornings, it seemed. I could hear it in his voice. I'd come out of my study far enough by then to detect these tones. I'd also been improving my eyesight. Stepping into the kitchen after everyone had left, I could see who wasn't there.

This was a kitchen we'd recently remodeled. Taking out all the white and grey, we'd redone the wood floors and gone crazy with color. Now, my countertops were tiled in all the same colors as my grandmother had dared to choose before leaving her kitchen--cobalt blues, spring greens, bittersweet oranges, and van Gogh yellows.

Henry Edward, Gwendolyn Rose, Willa Alice . . .

I didn't go around my house singing these names. Still, my children knew them. Like all those brown-eyed bundles Mom had clung to in in the back corner of our dead end, they could float. But I brought Willa further than I'd ever brought her older brother and sister when I saw her at her heat register.

"Here, Willa," I said, holding her hand and leading her back to my study. I pulled Willa onto my lap that day as I reached up to a shelf where I kept all the old faces. I'd never enlarged these old family portraits or displayed them prominently. I'd only kept them in a place where they wouldn't get lost.

"That's Ed," I said, pointing to a lean, short-haired, twenty-three year-old, sitting one step above me on a fall afternoon. Light was falling down through our bare branches that day. Looking at us, you wouldn't have guessed that we were a team. But we were just about to play some football.

"Oh," said Willa, "Where are you?"

CHAPTER 30

Connect All Corners

2009

"Maybe Grandma and Uncle Ned wanted to go somewhere warm, like Florida," Gwen said one night in reference to their shoe-shopping and taxi-taking times. By then, Gwen was a precise middle-schooler who had recently decided she no longer liked sleepovers.

With tight, dancer ponytails, she had an elegant way of swinging by my study before bed, asking, "What are you writing about lately, Mom?"

She was not just being polite. She actually thought I might have a new topic.

She was more patient with me and my perennial project than anyone else at this point, but she grew a little sweaty by the fire one Christmas Eve. This was a year when I had not only done some Christmas shopping but also wrapped a few presents. In addition, I'd agreed to a dog, which Gwen had systematically and painstakingly lobbied for since first grade. As a result, we now had a six-month old chocolate lab, Stanley, sprawled in the center of our circle.

Meanwhile, Gwen was crouching by the fire, tears beginning to fall.

"Whew!" I wanted to say like my mom whenever "breakdown" seemed anywhere near. But Bart and Henry were looking intently at Gwen. Even Willa, who had fallen asleep on the couch, was making a statement. With outstretched arms, she seemed to be saying that we needed to touch each other that night—that it was about more than simply sitting together.

In a rush of words, Gwen blurted out, "I feel like I'm whipping around in the wind and I don't know how much longer I can hold on."

She knew nothing about knot-tying at that age, but I immediately worried that I would soon be calling 911.

At seventeen, Henry was a long way from that time when he'd picked Gwen up in the kitchen and brought her to a warm, safe place. Even if he'd done some heavy lifting in his life, he still knew where he was going. Now, with the same forward-looking resolve, he said, "Gwen, this is what Mom's been writing about all this time. You need to get help *before* it gets worse."

Bart nodded his head. He told Gwen how he'd needed help to get me to see that I needed help. Now, Bart assured Gwen that we could help her get help.

Now, I knew the word I'd been looking for all that time in my study. I'd kept so much of myself and my dead end in there, thinking other rooms might not be able to hold it. But our family room had held *all* of us that night. Nothing had disappeared. Mom, Dad, Ed, George, Grandmother Bueckle and Grandfather Bueckle, all of my siblings and aunts and uncles and in-laws and grandparents, even my old trees . . . Everyone had kept us safe and showed us the way. We were *home*.

From left: June, Henry, Gwen, Dan, Willa, and Stanley in front, 2010

Age of Onset

1880 - My grandmother, Ella Petry, a surviving twin, is born into a family of opera singers, doctors, opthamologists, and milliners in New Jersey, where she suffers from childhood nightmares.

1910 - At thirty, Ella marries George Bueckle, an older, successful German immigrant, who has discovered "Salatan Solution" in Chile and opened The Sylvan Electric Bath Company on Schermerhorn Street in Brooklyn.

1912 - Ella gives birth to her first child, Gertrude.

1913 - After the birth of her second child, George, Jr., Ella takes a rest cure to Europe with her husband.

1924 - The last of three, my mother, Wilhelmina, is born.

1931 - Ella begins weeping in the living room of her four-bedroom house in Jamaica, Queens, allegedly over a portion of savings lost in the stock market crash. Over the next several years, she is brought to several private rest homes in New Jersey and, finally, Central Islip State Hospital on Long Island, where she lies on a bed and does not answer letters for the next ten years.

1931 - Gertrude takes over management of the household while attending Barnard College.

1932 - George, Jr., dies of scarlet fever during his first year at Rensselaer Polytechnic. Wilma is inconsolable.

1933 - George, Sr., slips deeper into senility. Gertrude becomes legal guardian for both parents. Wilma is sent to a small school in Greycourt, New York, where she has what she later calls a "breakdown" and cannot breathe on her first night.

1934 - At ten, Wilma is transferred to Noble School in Rye, New York.

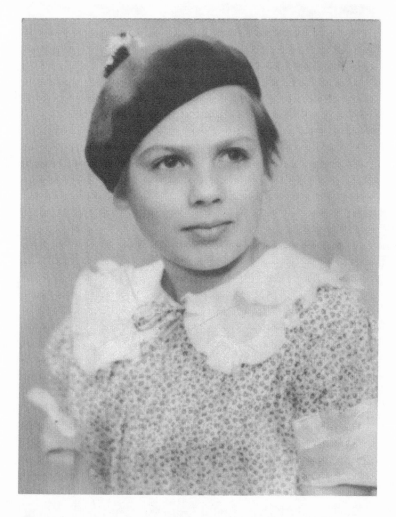

1935 - George Bueckle dies. His estate is valued at a significant sum. Gertrude moves the bath company to Columbus Circle.

1941 - Wilma graduates from Northfield Seminary (later called Northfield Mount Hermon School). Gertrude continues her affair with the family doctor, who has recently become divorced and a psychiatrist.

1942 - Wilma drops out of Guilford College, moves in with her recently deinstitutionalized mother on the Upper West Side, and meets Ensign Robert Edward Thiemann of King's Point Merchant Marine Academy.

1943 - Robert ships out. Three months later, Robert returns to New York and learns that Wilma is in Ft. Lauderdale, Florida, having suddenly joined the WAVES. He visits and they elope during her weekend pass. Over the course of the next seventeen years, they have six children, each of whom, at various times and in various ways, tries to venture further than the last from their dead end.

States of Ed

(from letters sent on the road, 1980-1984)

"Hi everyone—Guess who? If any of you haven't figured who this is by now you might as well hang up whatever it was you were doing and go back to school—not really, just kidding. ha ha Just got your letter to me today dad and is probably why I writing this one right now. I still here in Logan County Jail, this being a Wednesday, hope that's the correct spelling for the day of the week it is." — September 1981, Oklahoma City, Oklahoma

"Besides going to Clearwater and donating blood I've been try-ing to read a lot one of my goals in life is to read the holy bible and so far I am reading Genesis and learning quite a lot and having fun doing it. I'm in a Mr. Donut shop writing you and listening to the radio that's being played even though it's very early into the AM. I am feeling not at all tired and hope to stay up all night and rest sometime else." —January 1983, Lakeland, Florida

"I am planning on staying in this city for at least 2 months. I wish I could have come home while I had the chance with the bus pass but I did not want to displease anyone there at home and I am a little bit disappointed is all." —February 1983, Lakeland, Florida

"The folks here are nice and I'm really having a good time. I don't know where I'll go from here just yet. I am thinking about maybe heading north to some more tomato packers." —May 1983, Tomatoes of Ruskin, Ruskin, Florida

"Hi all, me just got out of PCJ (Polk County Jail) yesterday evening and me took a cab to Lakeland where me is at present. Well, well, well, it is real, real good to be gone from confinement in Bartow, Florida. I have yet to see and hear a worse group of cellmates. However, I did manage to get away from there without personal injury." —June 1983, Lakeland, Florida

"Hi everyone, hope your all doing fine. I'm alright and doing fine. I'm at my third fruit pickers." —July 1983, Johnston, South Carolina

"I have been reading the Bible in my spare time and have read the first six books of the old testament. I feel as though I could be in the 'peak of health' as Warren thought I might be in one of his letters." — August 1983, Massie's Mill, Virginia

Various Places Where Ned Could Be Reached:

Circa 1990s

Various Places Where Ned Could Be Reached

circa 1990's

Afterword

As it turned out, I managed to get everyone around the table again in the summer of 2010. This was roughly a year after Ned came up to my part of the country. He was all smiles when he arrived at Abbott Northwestern hospital on a warm, fall night, driven by the director and assistant of the "Willows," a residential care facility located on the western edge of our hometown where Ned had been complaining about the limited vocabulary of his fellow patients and throwing pills at the nurses.

Accordingly, the director thought Ned would benefit from a change of scenery and went so far as to offer up his time and black Ford Explorer for free. He was a nice guy, but he made the mistake of letting Ned out for a cigarette somewhere around Eau Claire, Wisconsin. Dad would've known better.

Eventually, Ned agreed to get back in the car, but it was well after midnight by the time he strolled into the emergency room. He was wearing khaki shorts, topsiders, and red, non-slip socks from another recent emergency room. I told him he looked like Garrison Keillor. Looking at the clock and gesturing toward the handful of people in the waiting room, he seemed to say, "It's showtime!"

A few hours later, we were in the examining room. I had mistakenly used the pronoun "he" when asked by the nurse why *we* were here. Once again, Dad would've known better.

Before that moment, Ned and I had been talking about Cervantes and Shakespeare. "Born under the same stars," Ned observed, pulling the words up from somewhere deep and bottomless like all those three a.m. nights under our trees.

Just then, a wind seemed to blow through our room . "She put me here!" Ned shouted, pointing at me. As the nurse went to get more security guards, Ned stood blocking the doorway, perhaps looking for a little protection, too.

From that night on, he bounced in and out of so many beds in my part of the country that it almost began to seem like he'd found himself another dead end. Finally, he ended up back in the hospital, where he tried even harder to return to his earlier state of coma. Remembering what Dad used to call "the royal treatment," I began bringing chocolate shakes.

Despite his shut lids, Ned seemed to sense my arrival on Station 47. In a matter of seconds, he would go from a fetal position to an upright posture and suck down the shake in one gulp. After enough of these shakes, Ned began to feel better.

Meanwhile, Bart came up with an idea to further cheer Ned. He proposed a family gathering for Ned's 56th birthday, which was still a few months out. Like Bart's other ideas, this turned out to be just what the doctor ordered. With a lot of advance planning, everyone made it up to my part of the country and around a few adjacent tables at an outdoor cafe one day.

Eventually, Ned made it to a modified Cape Cod overlooking a lake with a 24-hour staff that baked cookies. Now, on most days, he reads the *New York Times*, listens to music, watches foreign films, and opens his cell phone to pick up wherever he left off on that long and winding road.

Ned and me in my family room, 2013

Thank you, EVERYONE (especially in my own little corner of the universe) who helped me come out from under my trees and tell this whole tale.

Made in the USA
Charleston, SC
23 August 2014